Prayers
for Victory
in Your
Marriage

TONY EVANS

HARVEST HOUSE PUBLISHERS
EUGENE, OREGON

Interior design by Chad Dougherty

Cover design by Bryce Williamson

Cover Image © buravtsoff / iStock; Alex_Bond / Shutterstock

PRAYERS FOR VICTORY IN YOUR MARRIAGE

Copyright © 2017 by Tony Evans
Published by Harvest House Publishers
Eugene, Oregon 97402
www.harvesthousepublishers.com

ISBN 978-0-7369-6991-8 (pbk.)
ISBN 978-0-7369-6992-5 (eBook)

Printed in the United States of America

17 18 19 20 21 22 23 24 25 / BP-CD / 10 9 8 7 6 5 4 3 2 1

CONTENTS

Introduction 7

1. Love 19

2. Unity 27

3. Purpose 33

4. Forgiveness 41

5. Encouragement 49

6. Service 55

7. Communication 63

8. Spiritual Growth 69

9. Spiritual Warfare 77

10. Healing 85

11. Conflict 93

12. Sexual Intimacy 101

13. Blessing 107

14. Protection 115

15. The Holy Spirit 123

Dr. Tony Evans and The Urban Alternative 131

Thanks be to God, who gives us the victory through our Lord Jesus Christ.

1 Corinthians 15:57

INTRODUCTION

I f you are a believer and you are married, you're in a battle whether you realize it or not. The battle is for your unity to be destroyed, your love to be diminished, and ultimately your marriage to fail. Marriage is a foundational covenant created by God through which He manifests His presence and power in a unique way. Strong marriages lead to strong families. Strong families raise up a strong next generation. Satan would like nothing more than to do what he did in the Garden of Eden, tearing apart the family unit by inciting blame and undermining trust and respect. We all know what this led to—the removal of Adam and Eve from the garden and later the murder of one of their children by a sibling.

To say that spiritual warfare happens in the home is an understatement. The home, and particularly marriage, is a hotbed of Satan's tactics and techniques. Whoever owns the family owns the future. You can see why the devil would like to bring destruction to marriage.

The apostle Paul warned us about this ongoing spiritual conflict in several of his epistles, but perhaps most importantly in his letter to the believers in Ephesus, where he also spells out our strategy for winning the battle. That strategy has to do with the armor we wear as we enter into warfare with the enemy of our souls.

> Put on the full armor of God, so that when the day of evil comes, you may be able to stand your ground, and after you

have done everything, to stand. Stand firm then, with the belt of truth buckled around your waist, with the breastplate of righteousness in place, and with your feet fitted with the readiness that comes from the gospel of peace. In addition to all this, take up the shield of faith, with which you can extinguish all the flaming arrows of the evil one. Take the helmet of salvation and the sword of the Spirit, which is the word of God.

And pray in the Spirit on all occasions with all kinds of prayers and requests. With this in mind, be alert and always keep on praying for all the Lord's people (Ephesians 6:13-18 NIV).

In my foundational book *Victory in Spiritual Warfare*, I wrote extensively on how we're to engage the enemy with our armor in place. Now, in this second book of the Prayers for Victory series, I'm offering a collection of powerful prayers that address some of the major issues we face in our marriages. In addition, there are prayers for favor and requests for God to bless your home.

For each topic, you'll find prayers based on each piece of our armor. Pray these prayers word for word, paraphrase them, or use them as a starting point for crafting your own prayers. The main thing is that you pray. My goal is that these prayers will act as a starting place for you each day and that when the prayer I've written ends, you will go on praying in your own words about your situation.

The quotes before the prayers in this book are adapted from some of my previous books and used by permission:

Destiny (Harvest House Publishers, 2013)

Free at Last (Moody Publishers, 2005)

Kingdom Man (Focus on the Family, 2015)

Kingdom Marriage (Focus on the Family, 2016)

Life Essentials (Moody Publishers, 2007)

Marriage Matters (Moody Publishers, 2014)

A Moment for Your Soul (Harvest House Publishers, 2012)

The Power of God's Names (Harvest House Publishers, 2014)

Raising Kingdom Kids (Focus on the Family, 2016)

Victory in Spiritual Warfare (Harvest House Publishers, 2011)

Watch Your Mouth (Harvest House Publishers, 2016)

Remember as you pray that you do not pray as a beggar, but as a warrior for the King of kings. If you need help discovering what I mean by that and how critical it is that you claim your legal rights when you pray, listen to my sermon "Claiming Your Legal Rights" at go.tonyevans.org/prayer. You have power over your enemy when you pray. You probably have more power than you realize. Your task is to walk in your God-given authority so you are enabled to live out a strong and influential marriage. And you do that through prayer.

God created marriage with a purpose in mind—a mission. A kingdom marriage isn't solely about making you happy or making your spouse happy. A kingdom marriage successfully merges mission with emotion. Too often, couples lose sight of the mission and purpose while focusing on the disappointment of unmet expectations regarding their emotions. Then when happiness fades or the spark fizzles, they think that their marriage is over. Or their disappointment leads to conflict and complaining.

God created Adam and Eve with a purpose—to exercise dominion. *Dominion* means ruling on God's behalf in history so that history comes underneath God's authority. Simply put, the mission of marriage is to replicate the image of God in history and to carry out His divinely mandated dominion. That's why Genesis 1:26 says, "Let them rule." I go deeper into the dominion mandate in my teachings on marriage, but for the purpose of your prayers, know that the Lord has brought the two of you together in order to reflect His image on earth in the most holistic manner possible—through the union of man and wife—in order to advance His authority and rule from heaven on earth.

Happiness is a benefit of a strong marriage but not the goal. The goal is the reflection of God through the advancement of His kingdom on earth. Happiness occurs as an organic outgrowth as we seek this goal. Aligning our mindsets appropriately with the purpose of God can help us pray in connection with God's will for our lives, our relationships, and our homes.

The "Every Day" Pieces of Armor

Before we begin, let's take a brief look at each piece of armor. The first three pieces of armor are items we should wear every moment of every day.

The Belt of Truth   wear

Wearing the belt of truth involves realizing that truth is fundamentally God-based knowledge—His viewpoint on a matter, containing three principles:

1. Truth is comprised of information and facts, but it also includes God's original intent, making it the absolute, objective standard by which reality is measured.

2. Truth has already been predetermined by God.

3. Truth must be accepted internally and then acted on externally.

When you wear the belt of truth and use it by aligning your mind, will, and emotions underneath God's view on a matter—His truth—He will then empower you to overcome the lies of the enemy and fight your spiritual battles with divinely authorized spiritual authority.

The Breastplate of Righteousness   wear

Righteousness has been deposited within us. Our job is to feed it and nourish it with the truth of God so that it expands to surround us with the protection in warfare we desperately need.

✓ When you were first saved, God deposited deep within you a new heart containing all the righteousness that belongs to Jesus Christ. Righteousness is the standard that pleases God. But to benefit from its restoring abilities, you must dig down with the shovel of truth. Then God will release a brand-new you in your decisions and actions, and He will surround you with the secure protection of a breastplate of His righteousness.

Wearing the breastplate of righteousness involves walking securely in your imputed righteousness by virtue of the cross, coming clean with God in your practice of righteousness, and feeding your spirit with the Word of God so that the Spirit will produce the natural outgrowth of right living from within you.

The Shoes of Peace wear

A Roman soldier's shoes were called *caliga*—sandals studded with nails. These nails, known as hobnails, were firmly placed directly through the sole of the shoe for increased durability and stability. Similar to cleats worn on football and soccer fields today, hobnails gave wearers more traction. It gave them sure footing, increased their mobility in battle, and helped them to avoid being knocked down.

✓ So when Paul instructs you to have your feet shod, he is talking about standing firm. When Satan comes, he won't be able knock you off your feet. You will be able to stand firm because the hobnails on the bottom of your "peace shoes" have dug deep into the solid ground beneath you. Paul is telling us that we don't have to slide or move with every hit or trial that comes our way. Having our feet shod with the preparation of the gospel of peace gives us stability so we can resist Satan.

God offers us a peace that reaches beyond what we can comprehend. When we receive and walk in that peace, it settles in as a guard over our hearts and our minds. This is the peace that cradles people who have lost their jobs and keeps them from losing their minds. This is the peace that produces praise when there is no paper in the bank. This is the peace that restores hope in the face of failing health. This peace is so powerful that we're instructed to let it control us. We are taught to let it call the shots, make the decisions, and dictate our emotions.

Putting on peace shoes means aligning your soul under the rule of God's Spirit. When you choose to do that, God will release peace into your life because the peace of Christ is now ruling your thoughts and actions. When worry creeps back in, remind yourself that it's lying to you, because God has promised He will provide.

What can you do when peace in your life comes under attack? Take it straight back to the spiritual realm and focus on what God has to say on the matter. When you do that, you will wear shoes unlike any others. You will wear shoes that show the demonic realm, yourself, and others that you are standing firm in God's armor. You will walk without becoming weary, and in those shoes you will find the calming power of peace.

The "Take Up" Pieces of Armor

So far we've looked at three pieces of the armor of God you need to wear in order to be dressed for warfare. You wear these first three pieces all the time. The "to be" verb, translated "having" in Ephesians 6:14, indicates "at all times." We are always to have the belt of truth, the breastplate of righteousness, and the shoes of the gospel of peace.

The next three are what you are to have at hand, ready to pick up and use when you need them. Paul switches verbs for the next three pieces of the armor, telling us to "take up" the shield of faith, the helmet of salvation, and the sword of the Spirit.

The Shield of Faith   *have @ hand*

Faith is critical to achieving victory in spiritual warfare. Faith accesses what God has already done or what God plans to do. The shield of faith can also be called the shield which *is* faith because faith itself is the shield.

The Scripture is full of verses that describe this weapon of faith and show us where to find it. Hebrews 12:2 tells us that Jesus is the "author and perfecter of faith." In Galatians 2:20 we read that we now live by faith in Christ. "I have been crucified with Christ; and it is no longer I who live, but Christ lives in me; and the life which I now live in the flesh I live by faith in the Son of God, who loved me and gave Himself up for me." First John 5:4 says, "For whatever is born of God overcomes the world; and this is the victory that has overcome the world—our faith."

Faith is a powerful weapon, rooted in Jesus Christ. Jesus embodies all of the ingredients of faith, from its creation to its perfection. The key to winning in warfare is this faith.

I define faith in practical terms by saying that faith is acting like God is telling the truth. Another way of saying it is that faith is acting like something is so even when it is not so in order that it might be so simply because God said so. Your faith must always be directly tied to an action done in response to a revealed truth—otherwise it is not faith. If you are not willing to do something in response to it, even if that something is as small as simply being still in your soul rather than worrying, then the faith you claim to have is not real. Faith always involves your walk, not just your talk.

Keep in mind, though, that the weapon is not just faith in anything at all. It must be faith in God's truth. Faith is only as valuable as the thing to which it is tied.

For example, if faith is tied to your feelings—how much faith you feel—that faith will be empty. You might feel entirely full of faith but not follow up with actions because you really don't believe in what you say you feel. Faith is always based on your feet—what you do in response to what you believe. Faith is a function of the mind that shows up in your choices and responses to life.

The shield of faith has been given to us to protect us from the deceptive strategies of the enemy. When you use it properly, this shield will enable you to advance against the enemy because you will be confident that what God has said about your situation—through His promises in His Word—is true.

Pick up the shield of faith and grab the victory that has already been won.

The Helmet of Salvation *have @ hand*

With the helmet, Paul has once again used a physical example to illustrate a spiritual truth. He demonstrates that just as the brain is the control center for the rest of the body, the mind is the control center for the will and emotions. The mind must be protected with a helmet that's able to absorb being hit by the enemy and even knocked to the ground in the spiritual realm.

One reason we need to wear a helmet is that the enemy is trying to stop us from accomplishing the things God has for us to do. God wants to speak truth into our minds. He sits on high—in the heavenly places—and views the scene below. He can see the field of life much better than we ever could. He can examine the opposition's strategy much better than we can. He has studied the game film much longer than we have. And because of this, God has a few secrets He wants us to hear. They are secrets because often what God has to say to you is meant only for you.

Satan wants to keep us from wearing the helmet of salvation so that his whispers to us become the reality through which we interpret and respond to life.

Everything God is ever going to do for you has already been done. Every healing He will ever give you in your physical body has already been provided. Every opportunity He is ever going to open up for you has already been opened. Every stronghold God is ever going to break in you has already been broken. Every victory you are ever going to experience has already been won. The joy you're desperately seeking already exists. The peace you stay up at night praying and wishing you could enjoy is already present. And the power you need to live the life God has created you to live, you already have. This is because God has already deposited in the heavenly realm "every spiritual blessing" you will ever need (Ephesians 1:3).

Wearing the helmet of salvation means bringing our thoughts in alignment with our new identity in Christ, not our old identity in Adam.

The Sword of the Spirit ~~have a hand~~

This piece of armor stands out from all of the others. It's unique because this is the only offensive weapon in the arsenal. Everything else is designed to hold us steady from what the enemy is seeking to bring against us "in the evil day." But after God outfits you for battle in order to stand firm, He gives you an additional weapon with which you can attack and advance.

When Paul instructs us to take up the sword of the Spirit, he's letting us know that in this battle, the enemy will sometimes seem to be right in our face—just like a defensive player trying to block a shot in a basketball game. The defender will often stick his body, face, or hands in the offensive player's face so that the offensive player will become disoriented and unable to advance. Satan doesn't want you or me to send the ball through the net for two points, so to discourage this, he brings his battle—your particular stronghold—as close to you as possible. Oftentimes, that means your battle is being waged within you—in your mind, will, emotions, and body.

Paul tells us is that this is the sword *of the Spirit*. It's not your sword. It's not the church's sword. It's not the sword of good works or even religion. It's not the preacher's sword. This is the sword of the Spirit, and in fact, it's the only weapon we're told that the Spirit uses in the spiritual realm.

When you learn how to use the sword of the Spirit—which is the Word of God—you can go on the offensive against the enemy who seeks to destroy you. It doesn't matter whether you're young or old, weak or strong. All you need to know is that the sword in your hand is capable of doing more than you will ever need. You can follow the example of Jesus in the wilderness by using the sword of the Spirit to communicate to the enemy specific Scriptures that relate to your specific situation.

The Battle in the Heavenlies

Paul ends his discussion on the armor of God with a clarion call to prayer (Ephesians 6:18). Why? Because prayer is how you get dressed for warfare. Prayer is how you put on the armor. I define prayer as relational communication with God. It is earthly permission for heavenly interference.

Why does prayer often seem difficult to us? Because Satan seeks to direct us away from it. He knows how important it is. He will use every possible means to keep you from seriously communicating with God because he knows what prayer does—it activates heaven's response on your behalf in accordance with the will of God. Prayer never forces God to do what is not His will; rather, it releases from God to us what *is* His will. And it is definitely His will for His people to have victorious, purposeful, and loving marriages.

In the book of Daniel we find one of the greatest illustrations of prayer. We see Daniel studying God's Word and then responding to God in prayer based on what he has discovered.

> In the first year of [Darius's] reign, I, Daniel, observed in the books the number of the years which was revealed as the word of the Lord to Jeremiah the prophet for the completion of the desolations of Jerusalem, namely, seventy years. So I gave my attention to the Lord God to seek Him by prayer and supplications, with fasting, sackcloth and ashes (Daniel 9:2-3).

First, Daniel heard the truth of God. Then he talked to God about it. Anytime you talk to God about His Word, you are praying. You don't have to do it on your knees. You can do it while you are working, hanging out with others, washing dishes…whatever. Prayer in your war room is critical, but try not to neglect the need for ongoing prayer throughout the day as well.

Notice what we read later in the chapter.

> Now while I was speaking and praying, and confessing my sin and the sin of my people Israel, and presenting my supplication before the Lord my God in behalf of the holy mountain of my God, while I was still speaking in prayer,

then the man Gabriel, whom I had seen in the vision previously, came to me in my extreme weariness about the time of the evening offering. He gave me instruction and talked with me and said, "O Daniel, I have now come forth to give you insight with understanding" (Daniel 9:20-22).

While Daniel prayed, God responded. He sent an angel to help him understand his situation even more. Notice that God did not send the angel to give Daniel understanding *until* Daniel prayed in response to what God had already said. We read, "At the beginning of your supplications the command was issued, and I have come to tell you, for you are highly esteemed; so give heed to the message and gain understanding of the vision" (verse 23). When Daniel began to pray, God gave Gabriel the directive to go to Daniel and give him more understanding. The following chapter gives us greater insight into this occasion.

Then behold, a hand touched me and set me trembling on my hands and knees. He said to me, "O Daniel, man of high esteem, understand the words that I am about to tell you and stand upright, for I have now been sent to you." And when he had spoken this word to me, I stood up trembling. Then he said to me, "Do not be afraid, Daniel, for from the first day that you set your heart on understanding this and on humbling yourself before your God, your words were heard, and I have come in response to your words. But the prince of the kingdom of Persia was withstanding me for twenty-one days; then behold, Michael, one of the chief princes, came to help me, for I had been left there with the kings of Persia. Now I have come to give you an understanding of what will happen to your people in the latter days, for the vision pertains to the days yet future."

When he had spoken to me according to these words, I turned my face toward the ground and became speechless (Daniel 10:10-15).

When Daniel prayed to God in response to God's words revealed through Jeremiah, God sent a messenger to help Daniel. Twice we read in these two chapters that God sent the angel on the day that Daniel prayed to God about God's already revealed word. When you are praying according to God's own word, He hears you and responds. The delay in receiving that response was a result of spiritual warfare in the heavenly realm. Gabriel had been dispatched to go to Daniel with a message from God, but the prince of Persia—a demon—blocked Gabriel from reaching his destination for three weeks.

Your battle is fought in the spiritual realm. You must not fail to realize that. If you do, you will not fight in a way that will bring you victory. We've seen that God heard Daniel's prayer when he first offered it, and God responded immediately. Yet because of the battle taking place in the invisible, spiritual realm, God's response was delayed from reaching its intended destination. In fact, another angel—Michael—was needed to help remove the demon from acting as an obstacle for Gabriel. Ultimately, the prince of Persia got double-teamed so God's message could be delivered to Daniel.

Rarely is a battle overturned and won in a minute. That is why I want to encourage you to continue in prayer. God may not seem to respond immediately, but that's only because of the battles taking place in the heavenlies.

Each piece of armor has a specific use in our warfare against Satan. When put together, they present a mighty defense *and* offense against his tactics. As you use the prayers on the following pages to pray for your marriage, my hope is that you'll develop the fighting spirit you need to win the battle for your home and that you will join the mighty army of overcomers God is raising up. Your part in carrying out spiritual warfare on behalf of your marriage can change the course of your personal history, your family, your church, your community, and even our nation.

LOVE

The Belt of Truth

Love is patient, love is kind and is not jealous; love does not brag and is not arrogant, does not act unbecomingly; it does not seek its own, is not provoked, does not take into account a wrong suffered, does not rejoice in unrighteousness, but rejoices with the truth; bears all things, believes all things, hopes all things, endures all things. Love never fails.

1 CORINTHIANS 13:4-8

We often throw the word "love" around loosely, leaving it to be defined in many ways. People say things like, "I love chocolate cake," "I love football," or "I love that show." The words they really mean when they say that are "like" or "enjoy." The definition of love goes much deeper than what we feel emotionally attached to. To love is to compassionately and righteously pursue the well-being of another.

Dear Lord, thank You that You have first demonstrated to me what true love is. I don't have to guess what it looks like because You modeled it by giving Your Son Jesus Christ as my ransom. Love never shrinks back, and love is never selfish.

Lord, I pray that what I do for my spouse will come from a true heart of love rather than a sense of duty or the hope of getting something in return. When I serve my spouse in love from a sincere and pure heart, will You be kind to me and let me know You noticed? Will You reinforce this attitude in me by allowing me to see with spiritual eyes when my love makes a positive difference in my marriage?

Give me grace, Father, to love willingly and continually, even if I don't feel as if my spouse is meeting all my needs. Love is not conditional. Love forgives. Love believes. Love endures. Love never fails. Thank You for modeling that to me every day. In Christ's name, amen.

The Breastplate of Righteousness

Above all, keep fervent in your love for one another, because love covers a multitude of sins.

1 PETER 4:8

First John 4:8 tells us, "God is love." Since God *is* love, love must always be defined with God as the standard.

God is looking at how the fundamentals of a covenant are being honored in your marriage in order to respond to you accordingly. He is looking at the husband to see how he displays his love for his wife through his actions. He is looking at the wife to see how she honors her husband.

He is looking because He is going to respond to you based on your actions.

Father, there is no greater image or illustration of love covering a multitude of sins than that of Jesus Christ. It is because of His righteousness that my sinfulness is pardoned. I have been made righteous by His sacrificial love. I am benefiting every moment of my life and will continue to benefit into eternity because of Your love expressed through the love of Jesus.

I want to show greater fervency in my love toward my spouse, in gratitude for the love You have shown me. You are the standard. Not television, magazines, social media…not even my pastor or church. Your love is the standard by which I ought to love. My spouse is not perfect and makes mistakes and sometimes sins, but You have told me that love covers a multitude of sins.

Love offers grace where grace is needed. It helps me to keep my mouth closed rather than answering in anger when I feel wronged. Lord, empower me to love according to the standard You have set. Help me not to lower that standard to the level of those around me or even my spouse. You are my standard, and Your love is always faithful, true, humble, gentle, kind, forgiving, gracious, and powerful. May I love my spouse with the measure of love I have received from You. In Christ's name, amen.

The Shoes of Peace

I, the prisoner of the Lord, implore you to walk in a manner worthy of the calling with which you have been called, with all humility and gentleness, with patience, showing tolerance for one another in love, being diligent to preserve the unity of the Spirit in the bond of peace.

EPHESIANS 4:1-3

Love involves emotions, sure, but it also includes a conscious pursuit of good for the other person involved. Love's first concern is how does this action contribute to the recipient of my love's well-being? If it doesn't, or if it does the opposite, then it is not love.

Lord, You have called me to live with all humility and gentleness, to be patient and tolerant, and to preserve unity and peace. Sometimes I am able to do this more easily with others than with my spouse. This shouldn't be. I should be more humble, gentle, patient, tolerant, and peaceful in my marriage than any other place. But sometimes familiarity breeds contempt—or at least complacency. Keep my spirit alive and fresh with regard to my marriage. Help me to live in an ongoing attitude of gratefulness for my spouse. Let love be the defining atmosphere in our home.

I also pray for wisdom, God, on how best to cultivate peace in my marriage and home. I ask for wisdom about our schedules, entertainment choices, and work. Give us wisdom on how to interact with each other so that we promote peace between us. Place a guard over my mouth when I feel the need to say something that does not stem from a spirit of humility, gentleness, and peace.

God, I know this is asking for a lot, but You have brought us together in this marriage for Your purposes, and every day, every hour, we need Your hand to make us as useable to You as You have desired. Remind us of the power of peace. Remind me of the power of patience. Help us to honor each other and not take each other for granted. In Christ's name, amen.

The Shield of Faith

When I was a child, I used to speak like a child, think like a child, reason like a child; when I became a man, I did away with childish things. For now we see in a mirror dimly, but then face to face; now I know in part, but then I will know fully just as I also have been fully known. But now faith, hope, love, abide these three; but the greatest of these is love.

1 CORINTHIANS 13:11-13

Most people today view marriage as a means of looking for love, happiness, and fulfillment. Make no mistake about it, those things are important. Those things are critical. They are just not the most important, or the most critical. Yet because we have made second things first, as important as second things are, we are having trouble finding anything at all. Marriage is a covenant. It is a covenantal union designed by God to strengthen the capacity of each partner to carry out the plan of God in their lives.

Dear God, Your purposes don't always come to light as quickly as we like. I want to push the obedience button and then have You show me what it brought about in my marriage. It is difficult to love without seeing the fruit or results of that love right away. That's called loving by faith. Showing love while trusting You to bring about good is one of the greatest ways I can demonstrate faith in my marriage. Far too often I determine to model and live out the principles of love for a day or a week, but when I don't experience immediate results or fruit and I begin to feel taken advantage of, overlooked, or forgotten, I shrink back into selfishness and self-protection.

But You have reminded me that I do not see everything there is to see now. I do not understand everything there is to understand now. I am to give my spouse love in full faith that You will bring about good because You promise to honor those who honor You in obedience to You. It's easy to love, Lord, during a time of mutual affirmation, affection, or companionship. But in those droughts that every marriage has—every relationship has—that's when I must love by faith. Help me to trust that You will see and You will respond even if I feel my spouse has not. Empower me to pass the true test of committed love—to give in those times when I see no immediate reciprocation. Be my strength in those moments, enabling me to love with a heart as faithful as Yours. In Christ's name, amen.

The Helmet of Salvation

Greater love has no one than this, that one lay down his life for his friends.

JOHN 15:13

Saving involves sacrificing. Christ sacrificed for the church, and spouses ought to sacrifice for the benefit of each other.

Your spouse will know that you love him or her when you are willing to give up things that are important to you for something that they legitimately need for their well-being. It may cost you something. It may cost you time, energy, money, or a delayed or reduced achievement of a goal that you have, but that is because it is a sacrifice.

When King David went to make a sacrifice before God to petition Him to hold back a plague put on his people, he purchased the land on which he was making the sacrifice. He bought it even though it had been offered to him for free.

Why did he purchase it? Because he said, "I insist on paying you for it. I will not sacrifice to the LORD my God burnt offerings that cost me nothing" (2 Samuel 24:24 NIV). David knew that the nature of a sacrifice meant that you had to give up something in the process.

Lord, Your salvation came at great cost. Because of Your salvation, I live freely in Your grace, pardon, and love. Sacrificing for my spouse can sometimes feel one-sided. But that's what a sacrifice is, isn't it? Sacrifices are not about keeping score. They aren't done for reward or affirmation. David refused to offer You a sacrifice that cost him nothing because the very nature of sacrifice is giving up something for the benefit of another.

Lord, give me wisdom on where and how I need to sacrificially love my spouse. Show me ways in which I can improve in this area. Let me gain insight into the joy that comes through sacrificial love by understanding the joy You have in loving me, despite all it cost You. Salvation wasn't offered to me with a list of demands I would have to fulfill in order to get it or keep it. It came by Your sacrificial love. May my love for my spouse never be tied to demands or requirements. Make my heart soft like Yours and open to the pure pleasure of loving simply for the sake of making someone else's life better. In Christ's name, amen.

The Sword of the Spirit

Put me like a seal over your heart,
Like a seal on your arm.
For love is as strong as death,
Jealousy is as severe as Sheol;
Its flashes are flashes of fire,
The very flame of the LORD.
Many waters cannot quench love,
Nor will rivers overflow it;
If a man were to give all the riches of his house for love,
It would be utterly despised.

SONG OF SOLOMON 8:6-7

The words that were exchanged on your wedding day to promise to love, cherish, and honor each other were not just part of the ceremony. They were said in the process of making your relationship a legally binding covenant under the principle of two becoming one flesh (Mark 10:6-8). The ceremonial oath you made to each other is the public display of your marriage covenant before God.

Lord, love is powerful. The emotion of love motivates and inspires all of us. Its flashes are flashes of fire, and waters cannot quench it. Your Word speaks of romantic love in a way that embraces its power.

I pray that the romantic love between my spouse and me will be so deep, so great, so strong, so affirming that we will resonate with these words of Yours in the Song of Solomon. That we would be willing to give all our riches in exchange for love and not regret it for a moment. Help us to remember not to value our careers, our income, or our achievements more than our love. Within this love we find pure satisfaction—it is Your gift. Let us know it once again if we have lost it. Rekindle our flame and make our love as strong as death and our jealousy for each other's passion and interest as severe as Sheol. You are love. Fill us with Your presence and make us truly one. In Christ's name, amen.

2

UNITY

The Belt of Truth

The two shall become one flesh; so they are no longer two, but one flesh.

MARK 10:8

> One of the elements of God's rule is His heart for oneness, also known as unity. Unity can be defined in its simplest of terms as oneness of purpose. It is working together in harmony toward a shared vision and goal.

Dear Lord, unity in our marriage is about so much more than just agreeing on things. Your Word tells us that our unity actually reflects You to others. Our disunity reveals how far we are from You in our spiritual lives and character. Help me to keep a mindset of unity that is tied to the truth in Your Word, and not to view our decisions and disagreements as competitions of our thoughts and will.

Jesus described the purpose of unity when He said, "I in them and You in Me, that they may be perfected in unity, so that the world may know that You sent Me, and loved them, even as You have loved Me" (John 17:23). Unity is our way of demonstrating that You sent Jesus and that You love us just as You love Him. In Jesus we have redemption and the forgiveness of our sins, but our testimony is weakened when the most intimate relationship You have created on earth, that of marriage, is marred with disharmony.

Jesus prayed that we would be "perfected in unity." We are far from being perfected when we quarrel or hold strong to our own desires or decisions with no regard for our mate. Help me—help us—to be perfected spiritually through the sanctifying process of unity in our marriage. In Christ's name, amen.

The Breastplate of Righteousness

Make my joy complete by being of the same mind, maintaining the same love, united in spirit, intent on one purpose.

PHILIPPIANS 2:2

> Marriage is a sacred covenant, not just a social contract. God promised to bless the male and female and their offspring if they faithfully functioned in accordance with His rule.

Father, Your blessings and favor are critical if our marriage is to reach Your intended destiny for us. Yet Your blessings and favor don't come automatically to us simply because we are married. We seek them by living, thinking, and loving according to Your established plan. Help us to higher goals for our marriage than simply to bring each of us pleasure or to satisfy our needs. Help us to view marriage as the sacred covenant You intended it to be. When we view it through Your lens and with Your perspective, we will be motivated and inspired to live in a greater unity than we experience right now.

I ask that where it is my place to bend, grow, or be united with my spouse in a deeper level, You will give me the desire and ability to do so. Where it is my spouse who needs to do these things, provide the ability and willingness for that to happen as well. When we function together, being of the same mind, maintaining the same love, united in spirit, and intent on Your purpose, we fulfill Your kingdom agenda for our home. That is my prayer for us as a couple. In Christ's name, amen.

The Shoes of Peace

Make every effort to keep the unity of the Spirit through the bond of peace.

EPHESIANS 4:3 NIV

> Many husbands and wives work as a team to provide for the emotional, spiritual, and overall needs of their family. How beautiful it is when they bring that sense of teamwork home and model it for their children and for others in their spheres of influence.

Lord, unity takes effort. If it didn't, Paul wouldn't have written what he did to the church at Ephesus. He told them to "make every effort to keep the unity of the Spirit." Forgive us as a couple when we feel entitled to unity simply because we are married. Forgive me when I expect my spouse to get on the same page with me simply because I think I am in the right.

Unity takes effort. Effort comes in the form of humility, listening, grace, understanding, patience, and wisdom. Provide me with these virtues in a greater measure so I can do my part to work toward keeping the unity in our marriage. Provide the same to my spouse, and help us both to respond to each other with peace when the other has neglected these things. Let that peace be a reminder that our unity is a critical tool in Your hands to advance Your kingdom and to bring about Your purpose for us. In Christ's name, amen.

The Shield of Faith

Just as we have many members in one body and all the members do not
have the same function, so we, who are many, are one body in Christ, and
individually members one of another.

ROMANS 12:4-5

> Unity does not mean uniformity or sameness. Unity means
> oneness of purpose. Just as the Godhead is made up of
> three distinct Persons—the Father, the Son, and the Holy
> Spirit—each unique in personhood and yet at the same
> time one in essence, unity reflects a oneness that does not
> negate individuality.

Dear God, my spouse and I have some things in common, but we also
have a number of differences. These come in a variety of places, and
You know them all. Sometimes they are okay for us to handle, but other
times it gets frustrating. When I do get frustrated, I wonder whether
experiencing unity is even possible when we are so obviously different.
But You didn't say we had to be the same to grow in oneness. Rather,
our unity should reflect what Paul wrote in Romans, that the members
of Your body do not have the same function, but they are still one body
and members of each other.

Understanding unity and believing we can obtain it is easier when I
remember You are not calling me to be like my spouse, but rather to be
like-minded with my spouse, under You.

Where our spiritual perspectives and life views differ, please unite us
under Your truth. As we align our thoughts, beliefs, and values under
You, we will naturally be more united with each other.

Also, Father, help us to enjoy and make room for each other's differences and the unique personalities You have given us. Provide the
insight we need to understand that unity does not mean we have to like
the same music, events, or TV shows. Rather, unity means our minds,

thoughts, joint purposes, and morals are aligned under Your Word. When we live in faith, trusting in Your Word, we will be united. In Christ's name, amen.

The Helmet of Salvation

He is able also to save forever those who draw near to God through Him, since He always lives to make intercession for them.

HEBREWS 7:25

Unity occurs when we combine our unique differences together as we head toward a common goal. It is the sense that the thing that we are gathered for and moving toward is bigger than our own individual preferences.

Lord, through Christ's death and resurrection, You provided me with salvation for eternity. Jesus laid down His life to secure my eternal salvation. You paid the highest price for me—the sacrifice of Your Son. Because of this truth, I exist and am called to glorify You with my life. So is my spouse. We are not our own. Our purpose is to bring You glory through our choices, our words, and the state of our hearts.

Help us to relinquish our will and rights to having our own way as we seek to honor You in unity together. Give us the bigger picture of Your kingdom and remind us of our greatest purpose, which is to glorify You. Disunity is rebellion because disunity sets my desires and will above Yours. Disunity says I lay claim to my life, my body, and my choices with no regard to Christ's sacrifice and Your gift of salvation through the forgiveness of sins.

Unity reflects hearts of surrender under You, Lord, which is what Your Word says we are to do based on Christ's redemption of us. Give us this reminder when we experience discord in our marriage, and enable us to overcome the challenges we face in order that our hearts might be united in alignment under You. In Christ's name, amen.

The Sword of the Spirit

Now may the God who gives perseverance and encouragement grant you to be of the same mind with one another according to Christ Jesus.

ROMANS 15:5

> Satan spends most of his time trying to divide couples in their marriage. He does this because he knows that God's power and glory are both accessed and magnified through unity.

Lord, Jesus spoke these words: "Any kingdom divided against itself is laid waste; and any city or house divided against itself will not stand" (Matthew 12:25). I take up the sword of the Spirit, which is the Word of God, and rebuke any attempt to bring about or continue disunity in my marriage. A house divided against itself will not stand, so I refuse to accept and remain in a state of discord with my spouse. Father God, bring our hearts, minds, and spirits together where we have disunity. Your Word says we are to "pursue the things which make for peace and the building up of one another" (Romans 14:19). You have made it clear. We as spouses are to seek to say and do things that build up each other in You.

Give us insight and wisdom on how to do that. I don't always know what is going to build up my spouse in You. I may think it is one thing when actually something different would be more effective. So, Lord, please help my mind to be attuned to You so I will say and do the things that will truly build up my spouse in You. Let my words and my actions be prompted by You so we will be built up in You and united under You. In Christ's name, amen.

3

PURPOSE

The Belt of Truth

We are His workmanship, created in Christ Jesus for good works, which God prepared beforehand so that we would walk in them.

EPHESIANS 2:10

> Marriage is a covenantal union designed by God to strengthen the capacity and ability for each partner to carry out their purpose in the spheres of influence where God has placed them. Purpose involves impacting your world for good through fulfilling your purpose in all the places and ways God has positioned you to do so.

Dear Lord, You have designed each of us with a unique personality and skill set. You've also given each of us distinct passions and interests in certain things. All of this combined with our different backgrounds comes together to point us in the direction of our purpose.

God, help me to be a support to my spouse in pursuing his/her purpose. Show me what I can do to strengthen his/her ability to carry out what You have called him/her to do. I know You have a purpose for me as well, but I don't want that to get in the way of what You have created my spouse to fulfill.

When we pursue our purpose, we will experience challenges, setbacks, and discouragements. I want to be an effective sounding board so my spouse can talk about these things in a safe, loving environment. Keep me from trying to fix or question or change my spouse's challenges. Instead, may I provide encouragement and hope to keep going. Help me to be a blessing in my spouse's life so that he/she reaches the greatest fulfillment of Your purpose in their life. Keep me from selfish ambitions and selfish desires that may stand in the way of what You have designed us to pursue individually and as a couple. In Christ's name, amen.

The Breastplate of Righteousness

Do not be conformed to this world, but be transformed by the renewing of your mind, so that you may prove what the will of God is, that which is good and acceptable and perfect.

ROMANS 12:2

God has created marriage for the divinely appointed purpose of exercising dominion over the sphere of your world where you have responsibility and influence. As a couple, you are to influence those around you rather than be influenced by the world.

Father, You tell us that when we pursue You and Your Word, our minds will be transformed and renewed. We will then be in a position to discern Your righteous will for us. But when we neglect Your presence and Your Word, it is easy to be conformed to the unrighteousness of this world.

God, enable us as a couple to seek You every day in our conversations with each other, during prayer times together, in our text messages to each other...in any number of ways, help us encourage each other to renew our minds in Your Word.

We know that when our minds are attuned to Yours, the unrighteousness of this world will stand out. The world offers many things that grab our attention—making more money, buying more things, enjoying more entertainment—but achieving these things is not our highest purpose. Only Your purpose is good and acceptable and perfect. We seek to live by that standard and not the world's. Guide us into Your purpose each moment of each day. In Christ's name, amen.

The Shoes of Peace

Be careful how you walk, not as unwise men but as wise, making the most of your time, because the days are evil.

EPHESIANS 5:15-16

> Time has been given to you for one reason. Your time has been given to you in order to accomplish your destiny. Time is consistent with destiny and purpose.

Lord, Your Word tells us to be careful how we walk because the days are evil. The time to pursue our purpose draws shorter with each day. You also tell us to walk in shoes of peace. When we live with peace as a mindset, we can walk carefully. When we walk in peace in our relationship, we don't waste time arguing, fighting, or responding in unkind ways. So much time in our marriage has been lost to those moments when we did not choose to be careful how we walked, to use our time wisely, and to walk in peace. God, forgive us. Let that not be the norm moving forward.

Rather, I pray for myself right now, that You will teach me to number my days so I will be grateful for my spouse and the moments we have together. Teach us not to waste our time on frivolous activities that don't bring us closer to Your purpose, or on unproductive disagreements rooted in selfishness. Both of us have a great purpose to live out, so enable us to be time-givers to each other rather than time-stealers. And we will do this by choosing peace as the atmosphere for our home. When peace is the atmosphere of our home, we are freed up to pursue purpose more fully. In Christ's name, amen.

The Shield of Faith

The vision is yet for the appointed time;
It hastens toward the goal and it will not fail.
Though it tarries, wait for it;
For it will certainly come, it will not delay.

HABAKKUK 2:3

> Experiencing a marriage where both partners are fulfilling
> their purpose doesn't mean that every moment will be filled
> with bells and trumpets. It means that faith in God's calling
> and direction for yourselves, and for each other, will often
> have to carry you through those mundane moments that
> show up as a normal part in everyone's life.

Dear God, it's easy to question purpose and direction when things delay. It's especially easy if the delay causes any kind of discomfort in the home, financial loss of some sort, or inconvenience. All too often these delays can lead to doubt. And doubt can lead to division as we question each other and Your purpose in each of our lives.

Lord, help us to fully commit to seeing You carry out Your purpose for both of as individuals and for us together as a couple in Your timing. Give us the grace of patience when things don't seem to be falling into place. Help us to pick up the shield of faith and remember that the vision is yet for the appointed time, and until that appointed time comes, God, we are to serve each other in humility, encouragement, and mutual understanding.

When my spouse's faith diminishes because of delays and detours on the way to fulfilling his/her purpose, help me to be there to remind him/her to trust You in faith. And let my spouse do the same for me when my faith wanes. There are days when one of us is strong and the other isn't, when one of us is unwavering in our belief and vision of the future and the other's isn't. Help us to complement each other, to lift each other up in faith, whether by praying, or by speaking words of encouragement, or simply by not complaining when things seem to go wrong on this journey toward purpose. Between the two of us, help us to balance each other out so that our faith remains strong. In Christ's name, amen.

The Helmet of Salvation

God, being rich in mercy, because of His great love with which He loved us…raised us up with Him, and seated us with Him in the heavenly places in Christ Jesus.

EPHESIANS 2:4,6

God gave Adam a suitable helper to his need to carry out the instruction God had previously given, and that is to rule. God didn't give Eve to Adam just so he could have some company. God gave Eve to Adam so that he could have someone to collaborate with in achieving the goal for which he had been created.

God didn't fashion Eve out of nothing just so she could exist either. He fashioned Eve out of Adam's rib so that she could have someone with whom to collaborate in her divine purpose of dominion as well.

Lord, in Christ's death, burial, and resurrection, He secured for us a seat with You and Him in the heavenly places. The heavenly places are where our spiritual warfare is waged. Thank You for the power You give us through salvation—power not only for eternity but power to wage victorious spiritual warfare while on earth. You created us, man and woman, with the purpose of ruling in the domain and spheres of influence You have appointed for us. As a couple, we are able to carry that rule out even better than we could have on our own because we are here to support and help each other.

Remind each of us who we are in Christ and where we are seated, but also remind us who our spouse is in Christ and where he/she is seated. This will affect the way we speak to each other and honor each other, as well as our passion and motivation to help each other pursue our purpose from You. In Christ's name, amen.

The Sword of the Spirit

If you abide in Me, and My words abide in you, ask whatever you wish, and it will be done for you.

JOHN 15:7

> There are some wives who get an anniversary present every year. Their husband comes home from work, takes his wife out to dinner, gives her a great gift, and makes a big deal about that special day. But that's it. The wife doesn't hear from him in ways of love, affection, and appreciation for the rest of the year. But she knows that next year on their anniversary, there is going to be another great present, a nice date, and some kind words.
>
> Do you think those wives are satisfied with that relationship? Or do you think that they would gladly trade in an annual anniversary day for a consistent 365 days a year that were faithful and consistent and full of communication? Yet that's what so many of us do with God.

Lord, spending time with each other as a couple is a priority in our marriage, and rightfully so. But spending time with You in Your Word and in Your presence is critical if we are to have a victorious marriage and fulfill the purpose You have given to us. Help us, Father, to make it a priority to abide in You and Your Word. Help us to do this as a couple and also as individuals. We don't want to get so caught up in family, activities, and serving You and each other that we forget the importance of being still in Your presence and spending time in Your Word regularly.

You say clearly that if we abide in You and Your Word, we can ask whatever we want, and You will do it. You will bring us to our intended destination, satisfy us as a couple, and empower us to fulfill our purpose as individuals and as a couple. The key to living out our purpose is found in abiding in You and Your Word.

It is Your Word that will win our battles. The sword of the Spirit will cancel the lies of the enemy that entice us to give up pursuing Your plan. Your Word will give us wisdom to refrain from the distractions of our own flesh. Help us spend time in Your Word more frequently than we do now. Show us creative ways to do this, and we thank You in advance for both hearing and answering this prayer. In Christ's name, amen.

4

FORGIVENESS

The Belt of Truth

[Love] does not act unbecomingly; it does not seek its own, is not provoked, does not take into account a wrong suffered.

Forgiveness is first and foremost a decision. It doesn't begin with an emotion. It's not about how you are feeling at any given moment but rather about the choice you have made to no longer credit an offense or blame against an offender, even if that offender was yourself or someone you love deeply.

The best biblical defense for this definition of forgiveness is found in 1 Corinthians 13 where we read about love. In verse 5 we discover that love "keeps no record of wrongs" (NIV). That doesn't mean love justifies the wrong because to justify it incorrectly would not be love—that would be enablement. Neither does it mean that love ignores the wrong, excuses it, or pretends that it didn't happen.

What love means is that you do not keep a record of the wrong. This is similar to how God forgives us. He doesn't forget the sin, but He no longer holds the offense against our account. We are not held in debt to Him to pay off something that we are unable to pay.

Dear Father, I've carried around this weight of unforgiveness far too long. It's burdened my soul and sapped me of the strength and joy You have made me to experience. I've lost hours and days to bitterness, coping, and rehearsing the events of my past in my head. I don't want to live this way anymore. I know that it's creating distance in my relationship with You, and it's also causing friction in my relationships with my spouse and with myself.

Please join me on this journey of release. Open my mind and heart to understand Your truth. Give me the willingness to apply the principles and the power to forgive in my relationship with my spouse. Enable me to trust again, even if I do not feel my spouse is trustworthy. Let me be like Sarah in Scripture, who loved and trusted without fear because she put her hope in You. In Christ's name, amen.

The Breastplate of Righteousness

If we confess our sins, He is faithful and righteous to forgive us our sins and to cleanse us from all unrighteousness.

1 John 1:9

When someone wounds you and you choose to not forgive them, you lock them up inside a prison within your own heart. The problem is, you also join them there. In order to let yourself out of the confinement of bitterness and resentment, you need to let them out as well.

Don't let the weight of yesterday ruin today and tomorrow.

Dear Lord Jesus, I choose to trust that You are working things out behind the scenes for my greater good and Your greater glory. I can't have it both ways, saying that I trust You and then also holding on to unforgiveness. You allowed this thing or this pattern to happen to me in my marriage for a reason. I am receiving the benefit of what You are doing, so I accept the means through which that benefit has come.

Please forgive me for doubting You by hanging on to a vengeful spirit, pain, and bitterness. Pour Your grace into me so I can forgive freely, and open my eyes to see beyond the surface of my life to a deeper level where You are working all things out for good. Let my interactions with my spouse not be tainted by doubt, fear, or pain. Instead, give me the grace to love freely. As You have forgiven me fully and love me freely, help me to model and reflect that same forgiveness and love to my spouse. In Christ's name, amen.

The Shoes of Peace

Whenever you stand praying, forgive, if you have anything against anyone, so that your Father who is in heaven will also forgive you your transgressions.

MARK 11:25

When the wounds in our souls and relationships are left untreated, they fester and rot. They create residual pain in other areas of our marriage. Then even the slightest brush against this wound by your spouse—even if they didn't mean anything wrong at all—can cause you to react in ways you normally wouldn't. You may lash out, accuse, blame, cry, or say and do things you regret. All the while the other person is caught off guard by such an overreaction. In order to forgive fully, you need to treat your wounds, let them heal, and then take your focus off your scars by putting it onto your new start.

Dear Lord, sometimes I feel that I have forgiven my spouse, but then my actions or words reveal that I haven't quite gotten there yet. Thank You for being patient with me in this process and for reminding me that it is a process. Thank You for opening my eyes to see that my unkind words and my overreactions to things my spouse may do are results of harboring this pain and unforgiveness. I want to be set free, God. Help me to make steps each day that take me closer to completely trusting You and letting go of the anger and bitterness, the doubt and confusion that sometimes plague my thoughts. Set me free to fully enjoy the life You have created me to live and the fruitfulness that comes from experiencing the full manifestation of Your purpose in our marriage. In Christ's name, amen.

The Shield of Faith

Repent and return, so that your sins may be wiped away, in order that times of refreshing may come from the presence of the Lord.

Acts 3:19

> You may fear that what happened to you has so shattered or altered you that you will never regain the hope, joy, and delight you once knew as a couple. You fear that something that has been done or said has messed you both up too much, stolen your future, or your innocence. Yesterday is real. I am not saying that yesterday isn't real. What I am saying is that you need to stop looking at it so much that you miss out on today and thus dim the light of your tomorrow.

Dear God, things happen. Mistakes are made. Careless words are spoken. Trust is broken. Betrayal is felt. Indifference can grow. These are all parts of living as fallen people in a fallen world. When we live as closely with someone else as we do in marriage, we have a greater opportunity to experience these things. Over time, resentment, regret, and confusion may grow.

God, I do not want them to grow in my own heart or in the heart of my spouse. Despite what has happened, Lord, we must forgive. I must choose to view my spouse in the pureness of love that offers forgiveness freely. When I forgive my spouse's sins and offenses, times of refreshing may also come from You. Teach us both the importance and value of living with the fullness of a committed love that seeks to always forgive, always trust, and always show grace. In Christ's name, amen.

The Helmet of Salvation

If you forgive others for their transgressions, your heavenly Father will also forgive you. But if you do not forgive others, then your Father will not forgive your transgressions.

MATTHEW 6:14-15

When you don't forgive, you are telling God that you don't believe He had a purpose for that pain. You are telling God that you don't trust Him.

"Forgiveness" is a beautiful word when someone is giving it to you. It's a much more challenging word when you have to give it to someone else. But God has forgiven us of a debt we could never pay, and that motivates us to forgive others of their smaller debts against us.

You never want to burn a bridge over which you yourself will have to cross. You don't want to live in a relationally unforgiven state with a holy God because you refuse to forgive those who have offended you.

Lord, I know that the forgiveness You have shown to me is the model I am to follow with my spouse. You are wise and all-knowing, and You have a deep compassion rooted in Your understanding of all things. God, sometimes I cannot see past the pain. I cannot see past the offense. I cannot see into the purpose or beyond the event, happening, or unkind word. Lord, I am not all-knowing, and so forgiveness for me must be an act of faith—faith that You work all things together for good to those who are called by You and love You.

Forgiving my spouse is one of the greatest acts of faith I can do, but I can rest knowing that I am safe and secure in Your salvation. Your salvation is not only for eternity, but it is a daily saving of my mind, will, and emotions. I ask You to make Yourself so known to me at such a deep level that trusting You in this area of forgiveness will come naturally. Show me grace, God, and strengthen me in Your saving power so I can love freely and forgive fully in my marriage. In Christ's name, amen.

The Sword of the Spirit

"Pardon, I pray, the iniquity of this people according to the greatness of Your lovingkindness, just as You also have forgiven this people, from Egypt even until now." So the LORD said, "I have pardoned them according to your word; but indeed, as I live, all the earth will be filled with the glory of the LORD."

NUMBERS 14:19-21

If you are unable to unilaterally forgive, you are the one who is held hostage, not the offender. It has been said that unforgiveness is like drinking a poison and expecting someone else would die from it. But of course, you are only poisoning yourself. The bitterness, regret, and anger churning inside you poison your thoughts, override your emotions, distract you from living out your destiny, and jeopardize your relationships.

You cannot change what happened to you, nor can you change the person who did it. You can only change yourself and your response to the offender, so that is where you need to focus.

Father, Your Word teaches me not only to forgive but also to intercede. As Moses interceded for the people of Israel at a time when they needed it the most, I intercede right now for my spouse before You. God, forgive and pardon my spouse for what he/she has done wrong. Let Your loving-kindness be apparent in their life. Show mercy and mend what has been broken not only in their life but also in our marriage.

I cannot forgive in my own strength, and yet I need You to forgive as well. Let me see Your freeing forgiveness for my spouse, and let that serve as a model of how You want me to forgive too. In Christ's name, amen.

5

ENCOURAGEMENT

The Belt of Truth

Speaking the truth in love, we are to grow up in all aspects into Him who is the head, even Christ.

EPHESIANS 4:15

Most of us can think of someone who has encouraged us. Perhaps it was a parent, teacher, coach, or pastor. Few things are as meaningful as a timely word of encouragement that builds us up and helps us through hard times.

During my years of ministry, I have found that a voice of encouragement can be life-affirming, but a voice of discouragement can have a devastating effect. You must choose which voice you will offer to the people you meet each day.

As you encourage, always speak truth. In each and every situation, seek to discover the truth that will speak life into someone's heart.

Today, begin a habit of affirming the lives of the people you meet. Be an encourager.

Dear Lord, encouragement is such a gift when it is received. It is like waters flowing onto the dry desert ground, giving life and hope where there were none. I have received encouragement from You and from others when I needed it, and I want to be an encourager to my spouse. Lord, I try to encourage my spouse regularly, but sometimes I feel my words are falling on deaf ears. Help me not to look at the response to my encouragement as the motivation to encourage in the future. Help me trust that truth spoken in an encouraging manner will bring life. Thank You, Lord, for this gift I can give to my spouse each and every day. In Christ's name, amen.

The Breastplate of Righteousness

Encourage one another day after day, as long as it is still called "Today," so that none of you will be hardened by the deceitfulness of sin.

HEBREWS 3:13

On the days when you don't need encouragement for yourself, keep in mind that one reason you are placed in the body of Christ is to give that encouragement to others. Do it, because your day is coming. Disappointments have a way of showing up when you least expect them. They sneak up on all of us, so everyone needs some encouragement now and then.

How can you position yourself to receive that encouragement when you need it? It's simple—make sure to be an encourager to others when they need it. Always remember the "it" principle of Luke 6:38—"Give, and *it* will be given to you." The "it" you give away is the "it" you can be confident you will receive.

Father, I love receiving encouragement, and I want to apply Luke 6:38 by giving "it"—encouragement—on a more regular basis. Help me to have an open mind and attentive spirit as I look for ways to encourage my spouse. Give me creative thoughts about ways I can encourage that will truly make a difference. Make the giving of encouragement a daily priority for me and help me to see this encouragement bring life and joy to my spouse. Show me things in my spouse that I may take for granted but for which I should be grateful so that I may encourage my spouse to continue in these things.

And Lord, when I feel like complaining, remind me to reverse the complaint by offering an encouragement instead. Greed and complaining are sins, Lord, so strengthen me with gratitude and encouragement so I can stand firm against the schemes of the devil in my marriage. In Christ's name, amen.

The Shoes of Peace

Encourage one another and build up one another, just as you also are doing.

1 THESSALONIANS 5:11

> When you go through struggles, you need someone to come alongside of you and remind you that there is hope ahead. You need to hear a word to point your thoughts in the direction of God and His goodness again. So does your spouse. That is why we should always be mindful of this great gift we provide as we encourage each other when we need it the most.

Lord, when my spouse struggles and shares with me those struggles, help me not to take it as doubt or complaining. Help me instead to recognize where my spouse is at that moment and respond with encouragement. Let the words of my mouth always ring with hope and help. May peace rule in our marriage because we hold to Your command to encourage one another and build each other up. Forgive me for when I have done the opposite and torn down my spouse with my words. Help me not to do that anymore but rather to give words that inspire and point my spouse to a new level of faith in You. In Christ's name, amen.

The Shield of Faith

Consider how to stimulate one another to love and good deeds, not forsaking our own assembling together, as is the habit of some, but encouraging one another; and all the more as you see the day drawing near.

HEBREWS 10:24-25

So many believers in Jesus Christ fail to make it to the fulfillment of God's promises in their lives because they shrink back in the difficult or empty times rather than drawing near in faith. In times like these, we need each other all the more. Just as a toddler needs a mother to continually encourage her to keep trying to walk even though she falls down again and again, we need each other in the body of Christ to encourage us. We need reminders that we will one day reach the promises if we don't sit down and give up.

The word "encourage" means to come alongside to help, strengthen, or support. When would someone need help, strengthening, or support? When they are down, when they are discouraged, or when things are not flowing well in their lives. That is the critical time when we need to be there for one another. And when we are the ones who are discouraged, when things are not flowing in our own lives, we need others to be there for us.

Dear God, I desire to come alongside my spouse to offer help, strength, and support—especially with my encouraging words. I want to be there for my spouse not only in difficult times but also as a consistent, encouraging presence. Train my mind to dwell on positive and encouraging thoughts. Help me to exponentially increase the amount of encouragement I already give, Lord. I want my spouse to fully feel encouraged, and then I want to see what You do in their life for Your glory.

Where I doubt my spouse's thinking, help me to turn to You rather than complain. Where I question my spouse's choices, remind me to trust in You and encourage my spouse to seek You at all times. Thank You for reminding me of this virtue so that our marriage will be strong and will stand against the attacks of the devil. In Christ's name, amen.

The Helmet of Salvation

Each of us is to please his neighbor for his good, to his edification.

ROMANS 15:2

> The right word spoken at the right time can change anyone's trajectory in life. In fact, it can even revive life. Offering encouragement is like watering the soil around a droopy plant to bring it to life again. That's why it's essential that we stay connected.

Lord, I pray that You will make me an encourager not only in what I say but also in what I do. I see that encouragement is critical to building up my spouse, so I want to commit myself to doing this regularly. You have given my spouse great skills and a unique purpose, and I pray You will use me to encourage my spouse to pursue all You would have him/her to do and be.

Make me an instrument of good, life, health, and hope. Make the meditations of my heart about my spouse reflect this desire to encourage. Forgive me for when I complain and seek to put my own needs first. Remind me continually that love is the greatest gift I can bring to this marriage, and with love, You will do amazing things. Show me the fruit of my encouragement in my spouse's life. And, Lord, help my spouse to encourage me as well. Thank You. In Christ's name, amen.

The Sword of the Spirit

The overseer must be...holding fast the faithful word which is in accordance with the teaching, so that he will be able both to exhort in sound doctrine and to refute those who contradict.

TITUS 1:7,9

> We need to encourage one another in a spirit of love and truth (Ephesians 4:15). The best way to encourage someone with the truth is by sharing an appropriate passage of Scripture. Paul tells us in Romans, "For whatever was written in earlier times was written for our instruction, so that through perseverance and the encouragement of the Scriptures we might have hope" (Romans 15:4).
>
> Just like an excellent cheerleader at a football game is prepared and isn't just making stuff up along the way, excellent encouragers are familiar with the truth of God's Word and can apply it to other people's lives. They can bring hope through "the encouragement of the Scriptures." That is our greatest means for bringing lasting encouragement to others.

Lord, I want to use Your Word more in my life and in my marriage. Give me an increased passion and desire to read and study Your Word regularly. Help us as a couple to consistently spend time together in Your Word. Show us how this benefits our marriage. I pray You will empower me to commit Your Word to memory so it will fill the storehouse of my thoughts. This way I can quickly draw on Your truth to offer encouragement to my spouse in times of need.

Thank You for the gift of Your truth—a gift I too often take for granted. Let the thoughts in my heart be fully surrounded by Your words, for I delight to know Your Word and Your heart all the more. Let the spirit of encouragement bless our marriage in all we say and do. In Christ's name, amen.

6

SERVICE

The Belt of Truth

He called the twelve and said to them, "If anyone wants to be first, he shall be last of all and servant of all."

MARK 9:35

To serve is to focus on others and act for their benefit in the name of Christ. Service begins with a humble attitude and includes actively looking out for the interests of others. You become a true servant when you come alongside others and help them improve spiritually, physically, emotionally, or circumstantially. You serve when your actions make someone else's life better.

Dear Lord, one of the highest callings You have given us is to serve. Jesus modeled this time and time again—even grabbing a bucket and towel and washing His disciples' feet. Service reflects the heart of who You are, Lord. You give without strings attached. You wake me up every single day. You have made this earth and all it contains, and You sustain us, for You are the source of life. Service is Your normative way of being.

May this truth sink deeper into my soul. My service to my spouse should not be motivated by the desire to get something back. If I hope to get something back, my actions are more like business, not service. Service seeks to better my spouse and to bring You glory. Lord, increase my willingness to serve more faithfully and in ways that truly make a difference to my spouse. In Christ's name, amen.

The Breastplate of Righteousness

By grace you have been saved through faith; and that not of yourselves, it is the gift of God; not as a result of works, so that no one may boast. For we are His workmanship, created in Christ Jesus for good works, which God prepared beforehand so that we would walk in them.

EPHESIANS 2:8-10

When this passage refers to "good works," it's talking about servanthood. God has established and ordained opportunities for us to serve. If our Lord has prepared for us to carry out good works of service, we ought to be excited about fulfilling them. These are not random acts of kindness He has made us for. Rather, because of Christ's sacrificial death and atonement for our sins, grace has paved the way for the path of servanthood. Serving is one of the greatest and most tangible ways to give thanks to God for His gift of salvation.

The things that Christ secured for us on the cross— abundant life here and now as well as life with God forever—are to be the motivations for our service. It is the heart that drives the hands, the mindset that drives the movements.

Father, You have set the standard of righteousness for serving my spouse. I pray that You will soften my heart, lessen my pride, open my mind, and strengthen my feet to serve the way You have called me to. Before You created me, You laid out a path for me that included my marriage. You have endowed me with gifts and skills that can benefit my spouse. Use those to the fullest, Lord, and forgive me when I get in the way of their use. Guide my heart and mind back to You when I become selfish and refuse to serve, and help me to fully walk in the good works You have prepared for me to do. In Christ's name, amen.

The Shoes of Peace

It is God who is at work in you, both to will and to work for His good pleasure.

PHILIPPIANS 2:13

The canvas does not tell the painter what to paint. The clay does not tell the potter what to fashion. But many Christians are trying to get God to turn them into what they want to be rather than saying, "God, turn me into what You want me to be. You are the painter, and I am the canvas; You are the potter, and I am the clay."

Jesus is our model, and He said in John 4:34, "My food is to do the will of Him who sent me." His perspective is exactly the opposite from the one you're getting from the world.

When you are on God's assignment for service, He will give you the desire ("to will") and ability ("to work") to carry it out. God says, "I'll do the work on your inside and change your heart. You just have to do the work on the outside. Be obedient and listen for My voice."

Lord, one of the potential sources of conflict in our home and marriage is selfishness. When our selfishness trumps Your call to service, conflict will abound. You have instructed me to fight the enemy in spiritual warfare by putting on the shoes of peace. Those shoes bear the brand name of service.

I want to excel in this area, Father, so I ask You today to show me practical, tangible ways I can serve my spouse. Increase my awareness of my spouse's truest needs, whether regarding his/her health, emotions, confidence, or enjoyment of life. Make me the vessel through which You serve my spouse, and give me joy in the process. In Christ's name, amen.

The Shield of Faith

As each one has received a special gift, employ it in serving one another as good stewards of the manifold grace of God.

1 PETER 4:10

> When athletes want to strengthen their legs, they do an exercise called a squat. They put weights on their shoulders, bend low with their knees, and straighten back up again. With each bend of the legs, their legs become stronger. Do you want to know why so many believers are not that strong? It's because so few of us are willing to bend. Few of us are willing to go low and serve. We're unwilling to carry the weight of someone else and serve without expecting anything in return.
>
> God calls us to a life of humility and service. In order to live out His desire for us, we need to bend our wants, schedules, desires, expectations, and more in order to meet other people's needs. In doing so, we will bring glory to God while strengthening our own spiritual walk and faith.

Dear God, I pray that You would strengthen my service muscles. Give me the wisdom and insight to know how I can serve my spouse—and then give me the motivation to do it. In faith, I wholeheartedly embrace this call to service, knowing that I am pleasing You and deflecting the enemy through this act of faith.

Lord, when my heart feels used or taken advantage of, give me a reminder of Your love and faithfulness. Remind me that my spouse doesn't reward my obedience to You, God—You do. You are the ultimate motivation for all I do, so help me to keep my eyes on You, not my spouse, so I can serve my spouse more completely, regardless of what my spouse does in return for me. In Christ's name, amen.

The Helmet of Salvation

Before I formed you in the womb I knew you,
And before you were born I consecrated you;
I have appointed you a prophet to the nations.

JEREMIAH 1:5

The beauty of the gospel is that God says to every one of us, "I've got a plan and purpose for you." Jeremiah 1:5 confirms that. "Before I formed you in the womb I knew you, and before you were born I consecrated you."

God is mindful of us, and He has made a way for us to have fellowship with Him. He paid the price through Christ's death on the cross so that we might be saved. But that is only the beginning of the adventure. When we give our lives to God, we are called to do good works. God didn't take you to heaven the day you were saved, so He must want you to fulfill a divine purpose here on earth. The truth is, you were saved to serve. God has an assignment for you.

We've got to understand that when we surrendered our hearts to Christ, it was "moving day." Ephesians 2:6 says that God seated you in the heavenly places with Christ Jesus. You moved from a life based primarily on the physical realm—taste, touch, sight, sound, and smell—to a life based primarily on the spiritual realm.

The enemy will do all he can to keep you focused on the physical realm. "It's all about you. You're the most

important person. Climb the corporate ladder to get all
you can. He who has the most gold wins." But when we are
"seated in heavenly places" with Christ, we see we are called
to God's purposes, and that means we see life through the
eyes of a servant.

Lord, one of the easiest ways for Satan to defeat my spouse and me in
our marriage is to shift our eyes off of Christ and His atoning sacrifice
and onto ourselves. Satan will use things of this world to do this—full
schedules, everyday interruptions, a greater desire for material gain than
for grace…there are a myriad of ways to divert our gaze from the heavenlies to the physical realm.

Help me to seek You with a pure heart, Father. Do whatever it takes
to remind me that I am not of this world, that I have transitioned to the
heavenly realm, where I am seated with Christ. Help me to view all of
life from this eternal perspective so that my decisions to serve will come
from a heart of wisdom rather than duty. In Christ's name, amen.

The Sword of the Spirit

*Jesus, knowing that the Father had given all things into His hands, and
that He had come forth from God and was going back to God, got up
from supper, and laid aside His garments; and taking a towel, He girded
Himself. Then He poured water into the basin, and began to wash the
disciples' feet and to wipe them with the towel with which He was girded.*

JOHN 13:3-5

Just as He had done throughout His earthly ministry, the
Master became the slave. The Maker became the servant.
Jesus donned a towel, grabbed a bucket, and washed the
feet of those who in just a few hours would betray him.

This act of service may seem quaintly irrelevant in our
world, but in Christ's time, washing guests' feet before

dinner was standard practice. People wore makeshift sandals, they walked for transportation, and the roads were dusty, so their feet quickly became filthy in the course of everyday life. That's why a servant often positioned himself at the entrance of a home with both a bucket of water and a towel—to wash the feet of the family and guests as they came in. This was a common way of saying, "Welcome."

By kneeling and washing His disciples' feet, Jesus demonstrated what service ought to look like.

Because Jesus fully grasped His own freedom and significance, He was able to serve. Too often, we waver in our self-worth, and as a result, we jockey for positions of honor rather than opportunities to serve. But Jesus shows us the key to serving—His actions were rooted in an authentic identity with God.

Lord, washing my spouse's feet may not be an effective act of service today. But the meaning of what Jesus did remains. He did what a servant in His day and culture would do. Help me to have the mindset of service—to look for things a servant would do for my spouse and then do them. I want to grow in this area of servanthood because the more I serve, the more I am like Christ. Strengthen my resolve to serve willingly, continually, and fervently—not for the response, but for the joy set before me. I want to hear You say, "Well done, good and faithful servant." In Christ's name, amen.

7

COMMUNICATION

The Belt of Truth

Speaking the truth in love, we are to grow up in all aspects into Him who is the head, even Christ.

EPHESIANS 4:15

> One reason families break apart is the lack of honesty and a consequent lack of trust. People are afraid to tell each other what they really think and feel. They are afraid to be vulnerable.

Dear Lord, I pray that You will give me the grace and the courage to speak honestly with my spouse, even in those areas that may lead to friction. Please help me to couch my words in compassion and season my sentiment with salt so that what I say is truly heard. Also enable me to find the courage and willingness to be more vulnerable with my spouse. Help me to express my own fears, insecurities, and emotions.

May our love for each other create a safe atmosphere that promotes honest communication. Inspire us to offer each other assurance that honest words spoken in love are welcome in our relationship. Help us to grow closer to each other and to You so we can speak more freely and share our most intimate thoughts.

Thank You for the gift of my spouse and the gift I am to be for my spouse, especially in this area. Let our communication be a building block of our commitment to each other. In Christ's name, amen.

The Breastplate of Righteousness

The mouth of the righteous utters wisdom,
And his tongue speaks justice.

PSALM 37:30

> Most marital problems stem from poor communication. When a couple tells me in counseling about how they fight all of the time, they're actually saying that they don't communicate well. Good communication is critical to lasting and fruitful relationships.

Father, good communication is critical to my marriage. Please open up our hearts to desire an increase in our communication with each other. Let our words be filled with Your righteousness and with wisdom so that we can promote justice and equity in every situation.

May the words I speak to my spouse build up and not destroy; may they lift up and not tear down. I ask that You will guide and instruct my spouse in his/her speech as well so that both of us will bring about good in our relationship through our words. In Christ's name, amen.

The Shoes of Peace

Let no unwholesome word proceed from your mouth, but only such a word as is good for edification according to the need of the moment, so that it will give grace to those who hear.

EPHESIANS 4:29

Minimize the time spent complaining by keeping your communication flow open and ongoing. Deal with hurts and misunderstandings quickly, and then you will enjoy more times of compliments, praises, and making good memories.

Lord, complaining can lead to division in our marriage relationship. Yet there are times when one of us feels hurt, misunderstood, or disappointed. I pray that You will remind us to address these hurts, misunderstandings, and disappointments directly and quickly so they don't linger and steal the time we could be spending enjoying each other. Enable us to have the confidence and restraint to voice these things with honesty, kindness, and love. And give us the understanding and grace to recognize when we have hurt our spouse and need to make amends.

Thank You for reminding us in Your Word to use our words for edification according to the need of the moment. Use our words to give us life, guidance, and encouragement through each other. In Christ's name, amen.

The Shield of Faith

Truly I say to you, whoever says to this mountain, "Be taken up and cast into the sea," and does not doubt in his heart, but believes that what he says is going to happen, it will be granted him.

MARK 11:23

When God's Word—His rule, thoughts, and will—proceeds out of our mouths, we tap into a power source that is beyond us. We access and utilize the authority of the One who spoke the creation into being and commanded the waves of the sea to be still. His authority is available to you and me if we will but believe it to be true and speak directly to whatever mountain we are facing.

> The solution to the mountains in your life lies in what you say.

Dear God, issues in my marriage can feel like mountains at times. They can feel unsolvable—too high to get over, too wide to go around, and too big to remove. But nothing is impossible with You. You have given us a way to handle or remove issues in our lives when we have faith in You.

Lord, strengthen my faith with regard to the issues in my marriage. Help me to use my mouth and my words as weapons against the enemy in order to speak life, healing, hope, restoration, and forgiveness into my marriage. Let my words be used with the power You intended, rooted in Your truth. Help me to know what to say and what to believe so my marriage will grow and thrive. In Christ's name, amen.

The Helmet of Salvation

In the beginning was the Word, and the Word was with God, and the Word was God. He was in the beginning with God. All things came into being through Him, and apart from Him nothing came into being that has come into being.

JOHN 1:1-3

> When God created the world and said such things as "Let there be light," those words would not have carried any weight without His ability to bring them to fruition. In other words, God brings things about in reality by what He says. Before you see it, God said it. And before God said it, He thought it. Words are thoughts made audible. God thought it, He said it, and it was done.
>
> Since you and I are not God, we must begin with this truth: Have faith in God. Once our heart's desire aligns

with His perspective, whatever we say in faith can and will come about. This principle is replete in Scripture.

Our words carry weight when they are rooted in faith in God's will and power.

Lord, You spoke the world into existence. Your communication carries not only the power of creation but also the power of salvation. The Christ who was in the beginning with God and through whom all things came into being is the same Christ who secured my eternal salvation through His sacrifice. On the cross, Jesus refrained from speaking harshly to those condemning Him. He spoke only life-giving words, asking that You forgive them.

Lord, let my communication be as creative and as redemptive in my marriage. Give me restraint when I should be restrained. Give me compassion when I should have compassion. Help me to offer the soothing ointment of kindness in communication as well as the powerful, creative force of words spoken well. In Christ's name, amen.

The Sword of the Spirit

Having the same spirit of faith, according to what is written, "I believed, therefore I spoke," we also believe, therefore we also speak.

2 CORINTHIANS 4:13

Satan tempted Jesus in the desert at a vulnerable time in His life. Jesus was isolated from His friends, and He was weak and hungry from fasting. Jesus responded to the devil's temptations by having a Bible study with him. When the devil tempted Him to turn stones to bread, Christ replied, "Man shall not live on bread alone, but on every word that comes from the mouth of God" (Matthew 4:4 NIV). It is the Word of God—from His mouth—that provides the sustenance and power of life.

When Jesus spoke God's Word to the devil, the devil had to leave (Matthew 4:11). Speaking God's truth into life's scenarios forces Satan to flee. And we all know that Satan is at the root of every issue we face.

Lord, in order to use the Word of God against the enemy and against temptations in life, I need to know the Word of God. I pray that You will develop in my spouse and in me a desire to know Your Word. Give us a hunger for Your truth. Help us to spend time reading Your Scripture and getting to know Your attributes more and more. And let those words be on our lips and in our minds when the enemy or our flesh comes calling. Let them be a reminder of where our power and authority lies. With You, we are able to resist Satan's schemes and deflect the darts of the devil. Keep us closely tethered to Your Word, Lord, so that we can use it as an effective weapon of spiritual warfare, just as Christ did in the desert. In Jesus's name, amen.

8

SPIRITUAL GROWTH

The Belt of Truth

Grow in the grace and knowledge of our Lord and Savior Jesus Christ. To Him be the glory, both now and to the day of eternity. Amen.

2 PETER 3:18

Peter told us to grow in the knowledge of Jesus Christ. We have His book, the Word of God, to learn from, and the Holy Spirit as our Teacher. We have everything we need to put the ingredient of knowledge to work in our lives.

Dear Lord, the closer we are to You in our individual walks, the more we can reflect You and Your attributes to each other. Spiritual growth is such an essential part of life, and yet we can easily neglect it simply because we are so busy. Some call it the tyranny of the urgent.

God, please establish reminders throughout my day to connect with You—to spend time in Your Word, in prayer, in worship, and in Your presence. Please do the same for my spouse. Give us both a fire and a passion for knowing You—not merely knowing about You, but knowing You so well that we can discern Your voice and Your direction. Help us to experience You more fully and more intimately. As we do, this will over-flow into our relationship with each other because our marriage exists to reflect the unity of the Triune God and to display Your attributes to others. In Christ's name, amen.

The Breastplate of Righteousness

Blessed are those who hunger and thirst for righteousness, for they shall be satisfied.

MATTHEW 5:6

It is far too easy to get off track in the area of spiritual growth and seek spiritual knowledge for its own sake. Yet that's like a husband who carries around a boxful of letters from his wife, content to read them instead of using the insights they contain to deepen his relationship with her.

Father, You tell me in Your Word that I am blessed when I hunger and thirst for righteousness. You tell me I will be satisfied. I do not need to guess whether You will meet this hunger of mine and fill it with Your goodness. You have promised to do just that. So if I am not satisfied, it is because I am craving something other than Your righteousness.

Forgive me for the times I've gone astray and stunted my own spiritual growth through apathy, busyness, or desires for things of the flesh. I want our marriage to be strong, and in order for it to be strong, we both need to grow spiritually. Will You nurture and develop in my spouse and me a hunger and a thirst for righteousness? Will You convict us when we chase after things of the flesh? Will You help us stay on track in pursuing You in our quiet times alone and together as a couple? Thank You for these things and more. In Christ's name, amen.

The Shoes of Peace

These were more noble-minded than those in Thessalonica, for they received the word with great eagerness, examining the Scriptures daily to see whether these things were so.

Acts 17:11

Attaining spiritual growth is the process of God training us to consistently live from the perspective of the Spirit rather than the perspective of the flesh. Maturity in Christ includes looking at and reacting to things from a spiritual perspective, not through the eyes of the natural man.

God wants us to get to this place of maturity, to live as we were created to.

Becoming a mature believer takes time. You don't become mature overnight. A baby doesn't hop, skip, and jump into adulthood. The Bible tells us that becoming mature is a process.

This maturing process will continue for the rest of your natural life, but you can learn to consistently respond to things from a spiritual perspective.

Lord, to be noble-minded is to receive Your Word with great eagerness and to examine the Scriptures daily. It is to set our minds on things above and not on the things of this earth.

Increase our longing to read and understand Your Word. Open our eyes and minds to various study tools that can help us to grasp the full meaning of what You have made known through the Scripture. Help us as a couple not to be satisfied with merely attending church or doing a short devotional time with You. Rather, discipline us to regularly seek Your Word and study to understand it. Show us how to go to Your Word directly rather than always being taught by others.

Give us wisdom as a couple on how we can make time to study Your Word together, and help us use opportunities to discuss the things we are learning. You say that these noble-minded people in Acts sought Your Scripture daily. Help my spouse and me to be as noble-minded as they were, and help us to seek Your Word daily. In Christ's name, amen.

The Shield of Faith

Leaving the elementary teaching about the Christ, let us press on to maturity, not laying again a foundation of repentance from dead works and of faith toward God.

HEBREWS 6:1

In order for faith to work, it must be practiced. Faith isn't just believing that God can do what He says; faith is entrusting yourself to Him so He can do His work through you.

Don't let circumstances detour you from faith. Even when things look as if they might not work out, don't stop trusting God. Don't let doubt detour you. When doubt is holding you back, take it to Jesus, just like the man who told Jesus, "I do believe; help my unbelief" (Mark 9:24)— and Jesus healed his son.

Trust in God and His Word. He is with you, and He is for you.

Dear God, I believe that my spouse and I can grow to be spiritually mature in our faith, but Father, please help my unbelief. Help me when I doubt or when I compare myself or my spouse to others who look so much more developed and mature. Help me not to look back on my life and think that I should be further along than I am right now. I don't want to get caught up in the what-ifs of what could have been. Today is a new day, and that's why I'm asking You right now to increase our faith and our spiritual maturity.

Together, we choose to press on to maturity in our faith in You. And if one or both of us falls back, come for us, God. Come lift us up and put us on the path to maturing and growing again. Give us a heart that wants to encourage each other to grow rather than a spirit that criticizes or complains when we find faults in each other.

You have shown me grace and patience in my spiritual growth, so let that same grace and patience flow through me to my spouse. In Christ's name, amen.

The Helmet of Salvation

The grace of God has appeared, bringing salvation to all men, instructing us to deny ungodliness and worldly desires and to live sensibly, righteously and godly in the present age, looking for the blessed hope and the appearing of the glory of our great God and Savior, Christ Jesus, who gave Himself for us to redeem us from every lawless deed, and to purify for Himself a people for His own possession, zealous for good deeds.

TITUS 2:11-14

> Our goal is to know Christ, not just know about Him. A lot of people can give you facts and details about the lives of their favorite sports star or celebrity. But there's a world of difference between that kind of knowledge and having the person invite you over for dinner because you are good friends.

Lord, Your grace has appeared, bringing salvation to all of us, including my spouse and me. Your grace teaches me how to live righteously and honor Your sacrifice for me on the cross. When I live with my mind set on the blessed hope and appearing of the glory of God and of Jesus Christ, I am encouraged to grow spiritually. I am reminded to be zealous for doing good things for others, including my spouse.

I rest in the knowledge that the salvation Christ purchased for me and for my spouse on the cross can never be removed from us. But I also push forward in light of this great gift, desiring an even greater and deeper intimacy with You. Lord, I want to know You. I want to know what delights You. Help me to know You more. Help us as a couple to know You more. In Christ's name, amen.

The Sword of the Spirit

The word of God is living and active and sharper than any two-edged sword, and piercing as far as the division of soul and spirit, of both joints and marrow, and able to judge the thoughts and intentions of the heart.

HEBREWS 4:12

> A two-edged sword cuts on both sides, which means it cuts coming and going. The Word of God is so sharp and incisive that it can pierce to the deepest part of our being. The soul is your personality, the part of you that makes you who you are. Your spirit refers to the new nature that God placed in you at the point of salvation. The Word can sort things out in our lives even when we are so involved or so confused that our senses can't discern good or evil.
>
> In other words, the Holy Spirit can use the Scripture to help separate the stuff you can't separate on your own. If you are ready to cultivate an intense hunger for Scripture, you'll find all the nourishment you will ever need.

Lord, Your Word is the greatest asset my marriage has. It is able to reach the deepest part of my spouse and the deepest part of me. It can remove wickedness where we can't even see it and bring truth to light. Your Word must be in my thoughts, on my lips, and in my heart for it to work as effectively as it should. If it remains in a Bible set on my shelf, I cannot use it to experience the victory in my life and marriage that I desire.

I choose to commit myself to knowing and regularly memorizing

Your Word. Help me to find the best way to do that, taking into consideration my schedule, my personal learning style, and the specific Scripture passages You know I need the most. Please let my commitment be a model to my spouse that will encourage him/her to do the same.

I trust You to use Your Word to accomplish everything You intend to do in my own heart, in my spouse's heart, and in our relationship together. In Christ's name, amen.

9

SPIRITUAL WARFARE

The Belt of Truth

"No weapon that is formed against you will prosper;
And every tongue that accuses you in judgment you will condemn.
This is the heritage of the servants of the LORD,
And their vindication is from Me," declares the LORD.

ISAIAH 54:17

Everything you do interfaces with the unseen reality of angels. Unfortunately, we have to face the fact that Satan has forces at work in our world too. They have been given limited ability to work woeful events in our lives, but God is sovereign. Nothing that the enemy does can change the course of our lives once we have placed our feet on God's roadway.

You will sometimes feel as though you are in an all-out spiritual war, but you must remember that you're not alone (2 Chronicles 20). God fights for you. Your responsibility is to believe in Him and His eternal care for you.

Dear Lord, sometimes I react in the moment when attacks come at me. I doubt that You will right all wrongs or vindicate me, so I take matters into my own hands. But I will not do that any longer. I will stand firm in faith on the truth of Your Word that when I am in alignment under You, You will give me the heritage that is due me. You will give our marriage the heritage that is due us. You will never allow a weapon formed against us or against our marriage to prosper. We let it prosper when we take matters into our own hands. But no more! Those old ways are in the past, and I choose to put my trust in You and the truth of Your promises. You will vindicate me, and You will vindicate our marriage in holiness and righteousness and peace. In Christ's name, amen.

The Breastplate of Righteousness

Submit therefore to God. Resist the devil and he will flee from you.

JAMES 4:7

> Spiritual warfare is sometimes designed as a test to validate your victory in Christ. Temptation is Satan's attempt to defeat you spiritually. Ironically, the test and the temptation can be the same event. God can use something—a circumstance, a situation, a problem—as a test even if Satan is using it as a temptation.
>
> Your response to this event can be a testimony to God's power. Satan works to discredit your testimony and dishonor God. But remember, Christ has all authority over Satan, so you can have victory over those struggles and temptations each and every time.
>
> The next time you feel tempted, turn to God in prayer. Lean on His strength. Fill your heart and mind with His words, psalms, and spiritual songs. Claim the blood of Christ over your situation. Do these things and more as you see God show up in what you once thought was a losing battle.

Jesus, You have already won this battle. You have already gone through the pain, betrayal, death, and resurrection that were required to secure my victory over Satan. My submission to You and alignment under You cause the devil to flee. They cause temptation to turn around and leave.

Therefore, I pray that my spouse and I will humbly live in submission to You and Your rule over our lives. Let our words, thoughts, and actions conform to Your will. Give us the grace of humility to seek You and Your way in all we do. When we walk with You in intimacy, Satan must flee. Show us how to bring You honor by submitting to You in our own hearts and in our relationship with each other. I know that will bring You joy and will delight us as well. In Christ's name, amen.

The Shoes of Peace

Those who wait for the LORD
Will gain new strength;
They will mount up with wings like eagles,
They will run and not get tired,
They will walk and not become weary.

ISAIAH 40:31

Cultivating a godly perspective on spiritual warfare and our physical circumstances doesn't happen naturally. But one way to encourage this is through gratitude. Thanking God for His grace and loving-kindness instead of complaining about our losses takes a great deal of energy and persistence. We need to develop a mindset that looks for God's grace at all times.

An attitude of thanksgiving should dominate the life of the believer. Ingratitude is the mark of the devil. Satan whispers in our ears to make us think God has taken good things away from us, but God wants us to look at what He has freely given to us. "He who did not spare His own Son, but delivered Him over for us all, how will He not also with Him freely give us all things?" (Romans 8:32). We have so much to be thankful for.

Lord, how easy it is to get caught up in the negativity of life. Negativity, complaining, and fear permeate our culture. Watching the news, skimming social media, talking with friends, talking with my spouse…negativity can come through a variety of ways. Satan subtly uses this negativity to shape my thoughts toward the challenges I face in my marriage. But You say that if I wait on You, You will give new strength. You say that You freely give me all things, including answers to my prayers regarding my marriage.

Father, I choose to direct my thoughts toward gratitude and good regarding my spouse because gratitude wars against the enemy. Cultivate in my spouse's life and in my life a godly perspective on all things. Give us a spirit of thanksgiving so that our hearts may be filled to the brim with peace. Redirect our thoughts and our words so we will express thanksgiving toward each other rather than condemnation or complaints.

I thank You at this moment for my spouse and for my marriage. I give You praise and gratitude for the gift of my marriage and for the good You are doing in it and through it. In Christ's name, amen.

The Shield of Faith

Be of sober spirit, be on the alert. Your adversary, the devil, prowls around like a roaring lion, seeking someone to devour. But resist him, firm in your faith, knowing that the same experiences of suffering are being accomplished by your brethren who are in the world. After you have suffered for a little while, the God of all grace, who called you to His eternal glory in Christ, will Himself perfect, confirm, strengthen and establish you.

1 PETER 5:8-10

Before your feet hit the floor in the morning, make sure that you claim God's armor as your protection. His angels are all around you, but when you clothe yourself for battle with the belt of truth, the breastplate of righteousness, the shoes of peace, the shield of faith, the helmet of salvation,

and the sword of the Spirit, which is the Word of God, their
job is made swifter and surer.

Dear God, thank You for my faith and for teaching me to use it as a
weapon. Faith can cause the devil to flee. You say in Your Word that
when we resist Satan while remaining firm in our faith, we will stand
strong. Give me faith, I pray. Give my spouse faith. Give us faith as a
couple.

It's so easy to get distracted by life, whether it's work, family, entertainment, food, emotions…whatever. I confess that it's difficult to be
continually on alert for Satan's schemes, so I ask You to help us to be firm
in our faith. When our faith is firm, we can't be knocked over by every
wile of the devil and every roar from his mouth.

Strengthen our faith as a couple, Lord. In Christ's name, amen.

The Helmet of Salvation

*The Lord is faithful, and He will strengthen and protect you from the evil
one.*

2 THESSALONIANS 3:3

As an overcomer, always keep this truth in mind: You are
not fighting *for* victory; you are fighting *from a position
of* victory. Christ has secured the victory for you, and He
offers you this victory through the armor of God. The victory is yours when you are well-dressed for warfare.

Lord, You are faithful. You will strengthen and protect my spouse and
me from the evil one. I trust in Your saving power and grace. Forgive
me for forgetting that I am fighting *from* a position of victory rather
than fighting *for* a position of victory. The victory over the evil one was
secured for me and for my marriage on the cross when Jesus died and
granted us salvation.

Thank You for the powerful, saving life of Jesus Christ that gives not only eternal life but also strength and protection in this day and age. Will You remind me of this truth when You see me drifting from it? Will You help me to keep my thoughts in alignment with You? I trust in Your faithfulness and delight in Your love. In the power of Christ's blood shed on the cross, I rebuke the evil one and his attempts to divide, destroy, and devour my marriage. In Christ's name, amen.

The Sword of the Spirit

"Not by might nor by power, but by My Spirit," says the LORD of hosts.

ZECHARIAH 4:6

When the devil tempted Christ in the wilderness, he told Christ, "Command that these stones become bread" (Matthew 4:3). He offered a physical temptation to meet a physical desire for food. But Jesus resisted the temptation by calling on the Word of God, directly quoting from Deuteronomy 8. Jesus knew the Scripture so well that He could employ it to resist the temptation the devil was throwing at Him. He trusted in God and stood on the authority of His Word.

You must do the same. When you look to your Savior Jesus Christ and lean on the Word of God, the victory is yours.

Lord, victory in my marriage must come through the power of Your Spirit. I speak Your Word over my relationship—it is not by might nor by power, but by Your Spirit that we will experience all You have for us, including victory over the enemy. Demonstrate the power of Your Spirit in my relationship with my spouse, even right now, God. Give me a glimpse of the work You are doing to meet the needs I have with my spouse. The power is ultimately in Your Spirit, so in Christ's name I pray for a mighty wave of Your power to wash over my marriage.

I will not succumb to the lies of the enemy, who seeks to plant division, resentment, distrust, and apathy in my marriage. By the power of Your Spirit, those lies are destroyed. I replace them with the truth of Your Word, which says that love always trusts, always hopes, always endures, and always believes. My marriage is made up of this love—a love based on the authority of Your Word and the power of Your Spirit. Satan has no say in my heart or in my mind because I have set my mind on the things above, I have aligned myself under the truth of Your Word, and I have placed my hope in You.

Your Word tells me that those who hope in You will not be disappointed. I speak this truth over my marriage, my spouse, and my own heart right now. I choose to hope in You, that You will increase the intimacy, respect, adoration, and mutual love in my relationship with my spouse. In Christ's name, amen.

10

HEALING

The Belt of Truth

The LORD is near to the brokenhearted
And saves those who are crushed in spirit.

PSALM 34:18

Each one of us will find ourselves in a situation that seems much worse than we can bear. However, if our expectations are set on Jesus Christ and His providential care, we won't stumble at the thought of going through a time of trial. In fact, we'll have His hope to comfort us even in what appears to be a hopeless situation. If you feel as though you are in a horrendous circumstance, be still before the Lord. Seek Him in prayer and wait for His will to unfold before you. Don't rush ahead; He will come to you.

Dear Lord, You are near to the brokenhearted, and You save those who are crushed in spirit. I take comfort in this truth today, Father, and ask that You will manifest Your nearness to me in ways that I can readily sense. I trust that You are near because Your Word says so, but Lord, help me to be aware of Your nearness. Help me to feel Your closeness. Help me to absorb the healing ointment of Your love.

Father, I don't want to carry around this pain attached to my marriage, but it's there. I don't want to live under the weight of a crushed spirit, but it's there. Your Word tells me that a bruised reed You will not break. Lord, I've been bruised. Maybe it's due to my own sin in my marriage or maybe it's due to my spouse's—the cause doesn't matter. What matters is the healing that needs to take place. In both of us.

Make Yourself near to both of us. Restore in us a spirit of trust, delight, and joy. Hurt has a way of diminishing those emotions in any relationship, but we need those emotions to fully experience intimacy and love in our relationship because love is rooted in trust. Heal us, Lord, as You have the power to do. In Christ's name, amen.

The Breastplate of Righteousness

This you know, my beloved brethren. But everyone must be quick to hear, slow to speak and slow to anger.

JAMES 1:19

> Once you've surrendered yourself to Christ in choosing obedience in the face of pain and hurt, God will take the negative circumstances of your life and work everything out so that He is glorified and you gain a new sense of peace and hope. The back of every tapestry contains hundreds of knots and strings. However, the front is a beautiful work of art. This is how God views your life and how you should view it too—you are His masterpiece, and He will never give up on you.

Father, being quick to hear, slow to speak, and slow to anger doesn't always come so naturally. If it did, we wouldn't have the pain and hurt we have in our marriage. I want to obey You in these areas, but my emotions grow so strong at times. That's why I am praying to You right now to bring healing into my emotions and healing into my spouse's emotions so that we can obey You more fully and more readily. Help us to listen well to each other and to Your Spirit. Help us to forgive each other fully. Help us to walk in rightness with our mouths, our time, and our attention. To nurture our relationship so that healing can flourish.

Show me what I can do to help my spouse to heal from the wounds I have allowed or caused. And show my spouse what he/she can do to help me to heal as well. Give us insight into each other's heart on such a level that we speak healing words effectively and consistently to each other's spirit. Keep the wounds of the past from triggering more pain in the present. Help us to let them go, knowing that You have the power to restore our union wholly when we trust ourselves completely to Your care and align ourselves in Your truth and rightness. In Christ's name, amen.

The Shoes of Peace

I…implore you to walk…with all humility and gentleness, with patience, showing tolerance for one another in love.

EPHESIANS 4:1-2

Since the beginning of time, the one question that has filled the hearts and minds of men is, why does God allow us to suffer? We will not have an absolute answer to this question until we are standing in His presence, but we do know that suffering teaches us several things. First, God can use suffering of any kind to draw us into a closer relationship with Him. Second, suffering teaches us to be sensitive to those around us who are hurting. Third, suffering teaches us patience and endurance, especially as we press closer to Christ through the reading of His Word.

Lord, humility and gentleness usher in peace wherever they are lived out. As do patience, tolerance, and love. Yet pain and suffering often erect walls in our hearts that keep us from growing in those virtues. Lord, let that not be so with my marriage.

I lift up to You the pain and the suffering we have experienced, trusting that You will use them for good and not allow the enemy to use them for bad. Let them draw us closer to You in our hearts and minds. Let them teach us to be more sensitive to each other than ever before, comforting each other and preventing further hurt from happening unnecessarily. Also, let our pain and our suffering teach us patience and endurance as we draw closer to Christ and dig deeper into Your Word. In Christ's name, amen.

The Shield of Faith

My flesh and my heart may fail,
But God is the strength of my heart and my portion forever.

PSALM 73:26

> Too many people are bound by yesterday. They're shackled by their past mistakes or poor choices. Remember, you should always learn from yesterday but never live in yesterday. Rather, allow God to show you the bright new tomorrow He has on the horizon for you when you give yourself entirely to Him.

Dear God, help me let go of the past and exchange it for a bright hope for a great future with my spouse. Help me to let go of the things that have happened that have caused distance between us.

At times I feel as if I have no more strength to hope, Lord, but You remind me in Your Word that even if my flesh and my heart may fail, You Yourself are the strength of my heart and my portion forever. I need You to be that strength for me right now. Give me faith, hope, and forgiveness so I can heal from the wounds of yesterday. Show me what to focus my thoughts on that will please You and bring healing to my relationship with my spouse. Give me wisdom on what I should do, say, and believe that will make this healing possible. Help my spouse to heal as well.

I am not the only one who has been wounded in this relationship. Give my spouse the grace to forgive, the faith to trust, and an ever-deepening desire for me. Surprise us both with the level of healing You provide and the love we have for each other. In Christ's name, amen.

The Helmet of Salvation

Be kind to one another, tender-hearted, forgiving each other, just as God in Christ also has forgiven you.

EPHESIANS 4:32

Most of us think forgiveness is a good idea until we have to give it. Forgiveness does not mean approving a wrong or excusing an evil. The Greek word translated *forgiveness* literally means "to release." Forgiveness is your choice to release a person from an obligation for a wrong committed. In the New Testament times, the word was used when canceling a debt.

Why is there a struggle in our hearts to forgive what someone did? Because there is a bill out there that has not been paid. We insist on being paid, yet years go by, and the offender won't pay the bill. But God says to forgive one another because He paid the greatest bill—the bill of our sin debt—with His own Son. If we can be the recipients of such great forgiveness, we need to learn how to offer forgiveness to others. When we do, we discover that we are the ones who have been set free.

Lord, I need to forgive fully. Not just in my mind but in my heart. I want to be tenderhearted and kind to my spouse, but I need to heal in order to resurrect those emotions. Will You remind me to forgive—and keep reminding me until I finally do? Will You keep at me to forgive until I finally embrace it? Will You do the same with my spouse so that he/she will also forgive me?

I pray for kindness to return to our relationship on a regular basis. I pray that we would be tenderhearted with each other. I ask that You will make that the way we relate to each other every day. You can do this, I know. That is why I ask. The God who raised Jesus from the dead can raise kindness and tenderness in my marriage and resurrect a deep love rooted in trust, purity, and peace. In Christ's name, amen.

The Sword of the Spirit

[Love] bears all things, believes all things, hopes all things, endures all things.

1 CORINTHIANS 13:7

Most of the mistakes we make are caused by following our feelings. Feelings are very real, but the question is, are they right or wrong feelings? If you attend a scary film at night, you might have trouble sleeping because of the feelings of fear that the film evokes in you. This is true even though neither the characters nor the events in the film were real. Whether or not the source of the feelings is real often has little to do with how we react in our feelings.

As you grow in your walk with Christ, test your feelings against the revealed truth of His Word. Align your actions to the truth rather than responding in your feelings, and you will find peace, calm, and a life of stable wisdom.

Lord, I long to love as Your Scripture says to love. I long to be loved that way as well. Far too often, feelings get in the way of living out the definition of love that You give us in 1 Corinthians 13. That's why I've come to You in prayer right now. I've come to You to ask You to give both of us wisdom that is greater than our emotions. I'm asking You to give us restraint when we have painful feelings. Lord, I'm asking that You heal the hurts that would create even more hurts between us. Bridge the gap our pain has caused and fill it with love.

I commit to bear all things, believe all things, hope all things, and endure all things. I commit to love my spouse with the love that comes from above. I pray that You will also work in my spouse's life to bring about the same commitment. Help us to truly reveal not only to ourselves but to others the power of biblical love—the power to heal, restore, and make new. In Christ's name, amen.

11

CONFLICT

The Belt of Truth

Be on your guard! If your brother sins, rebuke him; and if he repents, forgive him.

Luke 17:3

How often have we told ourselves that we could forgive someone but never forget the offense? We may even have tried to forget what happened, but our efforts failed. The fact that the deed comes to our mind is not necessarily a problem.

If we remember those events in pain, perhaps forgiveness has not yet occurred. The problem is not that we remember but that the memory makes us bitter and angry. That's a warning to us that forgiveness must take place so we can be released from the bondage of these feelings.

Dear Lord, one of the root causes of conflict in my marriage is in this area of unforgiveness. Carrying around unforgiveness—whether because of something my spouse did toward me or something I did toward him/her—creates an atmosphere of resentment, touchiness, and distrust.

This type of atmosphere is a breeding ground for conflict to grow until our marriage seems to be ripe with it.

Lord, start with me. I choose to forgive my spouse for the hurtful things that have been done to me and for the helpful things that have not been done. I also choose to forgive myself for where I have missed the mark in our marriage. The truth of Your Word is clear—I am to be on guard. And I am to forgive. If my spouse repents, all the better. But as Christ demonstrates on the cross, I am also to forgive even if my spouse does not repent—and then leave the results with You.

Forgiveness is such a difficult thing to do because I feel as if I'm giving up my rights, my control, and even sometimes my dignity. Help me to rest in my identity in Christ so deeply that I am confident that my rights as a child of the King, my dignity, and Your control of my life are all intact, even when I forgive. I love You, Lord. In Christ's name, amen.

The Breastplate of Righteousness

All of you be harmonious, sympathetic, brotherly, kindhearted, and humble in spirit; not returning evil for evil or insult for insult, but giving a blessing instead; for you were called for the very purpose that you might inherit a blessing. For,

"The one who desires life, to love and see good days,
Must keep his tongue from evil and his lips from speaking deceit.
He must turn away from evil and do good;
He must seek peace and pursue it."

1 PETER 3:8-11

Many times, God allows us to face great difficulties or conflict in our marriage—not to hurt us or make us feel as though we've been left without any hope, but in order to teach us to turn our faces to Him and cry out for help. Never forget that He is omniscient and knows all about our every circumstance.

David wrote Psalm 23 as a standard of hope. It's a

promise that you can claim whenever you sense despair through conflict coming your way. It's also a testimony of what God did for David and what He will do for you. When the problems of life heat up and your soul becomes dry and thirsty, God will refresh you by leading you beside His still waters.

David was never separated long from trouble. He spent years running from King Saul, who turned out to be a madman intent on David's destruction. Sorrow, loss, separation from family members, and deep heartache were the building blocks of David's faith. And in Acts 13:22, God calls him "a man after My heart."

Are you a man or a woman who has a heart for God? If you are always rushing and running, it's time for you to stop and let go. Allow God to give you a cool drink of His eternal water. Then your heart will know peace.

Father, Your Word is clear and straightforward. We can resolve conflict and prevent it from boiling over if we will consciously choose to seek peace and pursue it. I do want to see good days in my marriage and to love life with my spouse, so I thank You for showing me how that is possible. You have instructed us to be harmonious, sympathetic, kind, gentle, loving, and humble. All of those attributes work together to calm chaos and clear conflict from our relationship. Increase these virtues in my own heart and in my spouse's. And when things go wrong, give us wisdom and discipline to turn to You and cry out to You for help rather than to argue, fuss, and complain at each other. In Christ's name, amen.

The Shoes of Peace

Blessed are the peacemakers, for they shall be called sons of God.

MATTHEW 5:9

Scripture says that when you sow, you will reap a harvest, and the harvest depends on *what* you sow and *how much* you sow. Once you determine what you want to harvest, you will know what you need to sow. If you want supernatural and spectacular things from God, you won't just sow ordinary seeds.

Lord, I desire peace in my marriage, so I am seeking to fulfill the truth of Your Word that says what I sow, I will also reap. Help me to sow peace in my own soul, my life, and my spouse's life. I am not asking that I stuff conflict or never disagree, but rather that my spirit will overflow with peace and understanding. When there are disagreements and hurt feelings, let our conversation be filled with peace rather than tension and anger. Show me how to set the model of peace in our relationship, and help my spouse to be drawn to me all the more as he/she experiences it.

Blessings are ours when we seek peace because Your Word makes that clear. We are Your children, and the blessing of Your power, presence, and peace is ours. I claim these blessings in my marriage and ask for You to help us live with a mindset that honors peace. In Christ's name, amen.

The Shield of Faith

See to it that no one comes short of the grace of God; that no root of bitterness springing up causes trouble, and by it many be defiled.

HEBREWS 12:15

How can you rid yourself of bitterness? Through faith that God can use all things to work together for good. Jesus said that whoever has faith the size of a mustard seed can move a mountain into the sea. Bitterness is nothing short of a mountain. As is conflict. Yet faith can address both.

Keep in mind, the power of faith isn't based on who you are; it's based simply on who God is. Your faith is as big as the God you believe in. Like David facing the giant, sometimes God gives you a bigger-than-life problem so that He can show you His bigger-than-Goliath solution. Keep your eyes on Him, and keep the faith. He is faithful.

Dear God, please heal our hearts and remove the bitterness that collects in our souls. Please restore the way for us as a couple to truly be intimate and enjoy each other fully. God, the past has a way of rearing its ugly head at the most inopportune times and stealing the joy we hope for in our marriage. I pray a hedge of protection around our hearts, minds, and lives, Lord, that You will stand guard to keep the past in the past and keep our eyes focused on the future.

Conflict comes when we let things boil over rather than live in the peace, trust, and love You have called us to. Please, God, I pray for myself and for my spouse that You will keep our hearts tender not only toward You but also toward each other. Remind us of the love that once fueled us. Remind us of the things in each other that first drew us together. Teach us and train us to delight in each other again, God, as a way of keeping unnecessary conflict away. And when true conflict arises and must be dealt with, help us to handle it maturely and with patience, giving each other the full opportunity to share how we feel and listening with wisdom and a heart that seeks resolution. In Christ's name, amen.

The Helmet of Salvation

Be angry, and yet do not sin; do not let the sun go down on your anger.

EPHESIANS 4:26

Paul tells us to have the mind of Christ—the mind that sees obedience to God as the thing of highest importance. Out of love, Jesus came to earth to be a servant and to obey the Father's plan, even to the point of death and separation from God. When He sweat blood in the garden and prayed that the cup of death on the cross would pass from Him, He asked that the Father's will be done. And He followed through in obedience, trusting that God's plan was best.

Lord, I choose to trust that Your plan is best, despite how things may appear in my marriage relationship. Every day is not always going to be rosy, so when conflict comes up, help me to keep my eyes focused on You and not on the conflict. In a spirit of faith through the gift Christ secured on the cross, I want to honor You in my response to conflict.

I choose to make myself available to my spouse to discuss what needs to be discussed. I choose to listen with ears open to hear what is truly being said. I ask for wisdom to discern the root cause of the conflict. And I ask for self-control not to get carried away with the issues that come up, but rather to focus only on the root cause, allowing the issues to be resolved as the root is resolved.

Anger blinds my emotions at times, Lord, so I ask that You will cover my spouse and me with the blood of Jesus Christ. Under that covering, send Your angels to wage war on our behalf in our emotions and circumstances. Let our marriage bring You joy and accomplish the purpose You have brought us together to fulfill. Please, God, let us be an example of what a godly, biblical, kingdom marriage looks like. In Christ's name, amen.

The Sword of the Spirit

When a man's ways are pleasing to the LORD,
He makes even his enemies to be at peace with him.

PROVERBS 16:7

People have joked that we could be really happy if it weren't for other people. People have a way of messing up our lives. The problem is, you and I are people too, and wherever we go, we keep running into even more people.

The slave Onesimus discovered that when you run away from some people, you run into others (Philemon 10-11). Do you know what I'm talking about? You change jobs to get away from troublesome people, and you run smack into other bad-news people on your new job.

We humans are here to stay, so we had better learn how to relate to each other. Fortunately, we have God's Word to guide us. Relationship is one of the most important topics in the Bible, particularly in Paul's letters to churches where people of all sorts were rubbing shoulders.

Philemon was a prominent person in the church at Colossae. He had a slave named Onesimus, who stole money from him and ran away. The punishment for a runaway slave in the Roman Empire was death. But Paul urged Philemon to forgive Onesimus and be reconciled to him as a brother.

Has anyone ever hurt or offended you? God tells us in His Word that you can forgive others because of your love for Jesus Christ and the forgiveness God granted you through His death on the cross.

Lord, there are times when it feels as if my spouse and I are enemies. I know that's not true, but things happen to give that impression. But You say in Your Word that when a person's ways are pleasing to You, You make even their enemies to be at peace with them. So the way to resolve the conflict in my marriage starts with me. It starts with me living a life that is pleasing to You. First and foremost, that means I need to love according to Your biblical standard for love. I need to forgive according to Your commandment to forgive. I need to speak with words that please You, and to think thoughts that delight You.

To ask for You to step in and resolve the conflict in my marriage without the willingness to let You work on me first is not productive. You have made it clear what I need to do in order to be pleasing to You. Continue to give me wisdom about what this looks like.

Lord, I give to You any negative feelings I have toward my spouse. I give You my anger, hurt, disappointment, resentment, jealousy, and more. Please take these things. I choose to put my trust in You—that You know what to do with them better than I do. Thank You, God. In Christ's name, amen.

12

SEXUAL INTIMACY

The Belt of Truth

I am my beloved's and my beloved is mine,
He who pastures his flock among the lilies.

SONG OF SOLOMON 6:3

> The Song of Solomon contains the Bible's most unblushing description of sexual intimacy in marriage. Chapter 4 describes the buildup to intimacy in detail, and the beauty of it is that you see the self-giving between Solomon and his wife, the mutual yielding of their bodies.

Dear Lord, bless our sexual intimacy and give us great desire for each other and satisfaction from each other. I yield my body to my spouse and surrender all that I am to my spouse for his/her pleasure and enjoyment. I also greatly anticipate being fully delighted in his/her body.

You have given us a beautiful illustration of sexual intimacy through the book Song of Solomon. Write another beautiful illustration of this great gift through my marriage. Increase our desire for each other and our understanding of how best to please each other sexually. Give us grace to communicate our own needs and to hear what the other person needs, and help us to respond accordingly. Thank You for giving us the beauty of sex. Make it a pure pleasure in every way. In Christ's name, amen.

The Breastplate of Righteousness

Marriage is to be held in honor among all, and the marriage bed is to be undefiled; for fornicators and adulterers God will judge.

HEBREWS 13:4

When we sin, the consequence is separation from God. When we sin, we break fellowship with God. Paul conveyed his struggle with sin in Romans 7:19: "The good that I want, I do not do, but I practice the very evil that I do not want."

Paul wanted us to know that he understood our struggle against sin and temptation. He too wanted the victory but would fall to sin time and again. And if it happened to Paul, it can happen to us. But there is a solution to the struggle with temptation.

The way we get rid of sin is not simply dealing with or focusing on the sin itself. That would be like being on a diet and deciding to focus on food all the time—it won't work. Instead, to deal with temptation we must shift our focus.

Rather than keeping our eyes on the sin, we need to turn our eyes to the Savior. As we focus on Him and not on our Romans 7 experience, we find the freedom to overcome.

Don't look at your sin. Look to your Savior.

Father, keep our eyes, heart, mind, and thoughts on each other in our marriage and not on temptations that show up at work, in our friendships, on television, in pornography, or anywhere else. I pray that we will both be so fully satisfied with each other that we will not give temptations a second thought.

I also ask that You will help me to stay attractive to my spouse. Give me wisdom on how to take care of my body in such a way that pleases my spouse. Show me what my spouse loves best in the area of sexuality and help us to discover a deep pleasure in this wonderful way of communicating with and loving each other. In Christ's name, amen.

The Shoes of Peace

Let his left hand be under my head
And his right hand embrace me.

SONG OF SOLOMON 2:6

> What a woman needs starts in the morning and not at night. What a woman needs starts in the kitchen and not in the bedroom. What a woman needs starts with her emotions and not with her body. When some husbands say they want to meet their wives' needs, they are talking about something far different from what their wives understand by that phrase.
>
> If a husband is really serious about meeting his wife's needs, he will talk with her more, he will compliment her more. He will still be dating her and showing her love when he has nothing else on his mind but an expression of affection.

Lord, help us as a married couple to always continue cultivating our romance. Sex without romance is merely an action, an activity of release. But romance brings a level of oneness and enjoyment into our sexual life together that makes it all the more desirable.

I pray that You will enable me to fully and regularly engage my spouse in the areas of esteem, service, edification, and more. And encourage my spouse to do the same with me. May our sexual relationship together be a natural outgrowth of our daily life. May it be something that often brings us immense joy. Bless our physical intimacy so that we will be drawn to each other with such a deep, romantic passion that we will thoroughly enjoy and maximize this gift You have given us. In Christ's name, amen.

The Shield of Faith

Your lips, my bride, drip honey;
Honey and milk are under your tongue,
And the fragrance of your garments is like the fragrance of Lebanon.

SONG OF SOLOMON 4:11

The intimacy recorded for us in Song of Solomon begins with Solomon's compliments and words of admiration and appreciation for his bride, not with the physical act of sex. But when the moment of intimacy occurs, God Himself invites the lovers to enjoy one another. When this kind of intimacy occurs within marriage, God blesses it. In fact, God so believes in this kind of marital intimacy that He recorded it, detail for detail, in the Bible.

Dear God, the attraction and desire recorded for us in Song of Solomon is deep. It covers more than physical intimacy alone. It goes into conversation, longing, pursuit, compliments, patience, and so many aspects of the relationship between these two individuals.

I ask You to pour these emotions, thoughts, and experiences into my marriage. Light a spark that sets a fire ablaze in the area of sexual intimacy in my relationship with my spouse. Fill my mind with thoughts of my lover and fill his/her mind with thoughts of me. Increase our desire for each other and satisfaction in each other. Give us the full experience of this shared love. Fill us with faith in You to do all of this and more in our marriage. In Christ's name, amen.

The Helmet of Salvation

His mouth is full of sweetness.
And he is wholly desirable.
This is my beloved and this is my friend,
O daughters of Jerusalem.

Song of Solomon 5:16

> Sex was never designed to simply be a mechanism for biological fulfillment. It was not simply designed to address the problem of raging testosterone or elevated hormones. Sex was designed both to inaugurate a covenant and to renew it.
>
> The closest things in the Bible to sex, as a corollary to the covenant, are baptism and communion. Baptism is the initial public act you take before witnesses to validate your desire to be wedded to Jesus Christ. And communion is the ongoing action you take that, as often as you do it, renews this commitment to the covenant.

Lord, thank You for the committed, saving love of Jesus Christ and the covenant of salvation. Thank You for modeling what sacrificial love truly looks like. Help me to embody that love with my spouse and go further than I may feel at any given moment in order to truly meet the needs of my spouse—whether they are emotional or physical. As I rest in Christ, let my spouse fully rest in trusting me in this area of sexuality. Calm any fears of immorality or disinterest or rejection. Give us both confidence in each other and a peace with each other that honors our sexual union and marriage covenant in all ways. In Christ's name, amen.

The Sword of the Spirit

For this reason a man shall leave his father and his mother, and be joined to his wife; and they shall become one flesh.

Genesis 2:24

The Hebrew word used the first time Scripture talks about sexual intimacy is the word *yada*. It is the same word used when describing that Adam's and Eve's eyes had been opened and they "knew" that they are naked. It is also the same word used when we read, "Then the LORD God said, 'Behold, the man has become like one of Us, *knowing* good and evil'" (Genesis 3:22).

The word *yada* is not a word referring to body parts or physical activity. In all definitions of the word *yada,* which occurs over 1000 times in the Old Testament, it means to know someone, to be made known, to reveal oneself, and to know by experience. It indicates plumbing the depths of the reality of another person—or even plumbing the depths of the reality of God Himself.

Lord, thank You for making me one flesh with my spouse. Thank You for giving us the gift of sex as an expression of this one flesh. Help us to explore all of the ways we can benefit from this gift. Open our hearts and our minds to creativity and love with each other. Guide us into new ways of expressing our love for each other. Show us where we can find time in busy schedules to satisfy each other. Increase our interest and desire and allow us to know each other fully and deeply. You are the Creator of all good things, and You have given us a beautiful thing in sexual intimacy. Thank You for allowing us this pleasure in our marriage and this way to know each other fully. In Christ's name, amen.

13

BLESSING

The Belt of Truth

Every good thing given and every perfect gift is from above, coming down from the Father of lights, with whom there is no variation or shifting shadow.

JAMES 1:17

What looks like a closed door to you could be God's pathway to blessing. What appears to be a nightmare can become His dream for your marriage. And what may seem like the worst news you could possibly receive can actually be the point of a new beginning. This is because whatever God allows to touch your life is part of His plan for your future.

It's easy to think of God's goodness in a lighthearted way when everything seems to be going well in your relationship—a good job, health, a growing family, two new cars in the garage, and a house with several bedrooms. Life seems rich and full. But if you never learn to say "thank you" to the Lord, regardless of your circumstances, you haven't learned the truth of James 1:17.

Dear Lord, every good thing given and every perfect gift is from You. It comes down to us directly from You. There is no sin in You. There is no deceit in You. There is no trickery, withholding, or accusation. Jesus Christ has paid the price for all condemnation, and we are hidden in Him through the covering of His blood.

Standing in that truth, Father, I boldly ask You to bless my marriage. I urge You to give us all good things that You have for us. I ask You to pour down Your blessings, not in a sprinkle but in a downpour. Shower us with Your blessings and favor, Lord. And let that start with a spirit that is in alignment with You. With a relationship that takes joy mutually in You. Bless us, indeed. Place Your hand of favor upon us and expand our borders, Lord. For Your name's sake. In Christ's name, amen.

The Breastplate of Righteousness

The LORD God is a sun and shield;
The LORD gives grace and glory;
No good thing does He withhold from those who walk uprightly.

PSALM 84:11

Christ's life in us is the source of our hope. Emotional strongholds—anger, guilt, shame, depression, bitterness, discouragement, frustration, inferiority, low self-esteem, and the like—hold far too many Christians hostage. In many cases, we've forgotten that God's mercy is given to us freely. In fact, in His grace—His unmerited favor—He brings us face-to-face with the cross, where we receive freedom from each one of these strongholds.

What does this have to do with emotional strongholds? *Everything.* When you love God with all of your heart, you'll want to please Him and live your life for Him alone. There won't be room for bitterness, anger, or discouragement in your heart because you'll realize that these emotions are

counterproductive to the life that God wants you to live—
an abundant life overflowing with His blessings.

Father, You are a sun and a shield. You give grace and glory. No good thing do You withhold from those who walk uprightly. Look down from heaven on my marriage, God, and replace the negatives with Your positives. Replace doubt with trust. Replace bitterness with affection. Replace anger with love. Replace apathy with attraction.

You are the miracle-working God, so I ask in faith that You will bless us continually with good things. Those may include things we enjoy or vacations we take, but Lord, the truly great things in life are contentment, satisfaction, fun, happiness, and peace. Also purpose, Lord. Give us these things in such an abundance that we marvel at what You have done. Show off Your goodness through us and our marriage by blessing us and enabling us to walk rightly with You. In Christ's name, amen.

The Shoes of Peace

The LORD bless you, and keep you;
The LORD make His face shine on you,
And be gracious to you;
The LORD lift up His countenance on you,
And give you peace.

NUMBERS 6:24-26

What blessings will God give you when you honor Him? The definition of *blessing* is the enjoyment of God's divine favor. Blessing isn't just about having more stuff. It's a function of stewardship—using and enjoying the stuff you have. Remember, blessings aren't necessarily material things.

If you're serving God and valuing Him above all else, you don't need to worry about anything—God will take care of you.

Lord, bless us and keep us. Make Your face shine on us. Be gracious to us. Lift up Your countenance on us, and give us Your peace. Bless us with rest, contentment, and joy. Bless us with special times together when we aren't bothered by the demands of everyday life. Bless us with communication that edifies and strengthens us. Bless us with mutual interests and hobbies we can enjoy together. Bless us in our expressions of love, in our physical intimacy, and in our commitment to each other. Bless us abundantly with purpose, meaning, and pleasure.

Bless us with Your presence. Bless us with financial security. Bless us by making us a blessing to others. Bless us with a hope and trust rooted in You. Bless us with a wonder for life, just as we had when we were kids. Bless us with the ability to see things we should be grateful for rather than to focus on things to complain about. Bless us with good health, energy, and stamina for life. Bless us, O Lord; bless our marriage with peace. In Christ's name, amen.

The Shield of Faith

Now to Him who is able to do far more abundantly beyond all that we ask or think, according to the power that works within us, to Him be the glory in the church and in Christ Jesus to all generations forever and ever. Amen.

EPHESIANS 3:20-21

In Matthew 13:58 we read, "He did not do many miracles there because of their unbelief." Without faith, the blessings that God has for you in the invisible realm will never be yours in the visible realm. Faith is to be a way of living. You demonstrate faith not by what you say but by what you do. Faith shows up in your feet, not just in your feelings. That is why Paul instructed us to walk by faith, not to talk by faith. Faith is an action.

Dear God, correct us where we need to change—where we are demonstrating a lack of faith by our actions. We want to please You, Lord, so help us to live out our faith in its fullness. Your blessings are life itself, so help us to trust You for them, shielded by faith against the darts of the enemy who seeks to steal our trust, affection, and joy. Help us to be filled with faith. You brought us together in this marriage, so You have a purpose to fulfill, and You will bless us in it. In Christ's name, amen.

The Helmet of Salvation

Blessed be the God and Father of our Lord Jesus Christ, who has blessed us with every spiritual blessing in the heavenly places in Christ.

EPHESIANS 1:3

God honors those who honor Him, and God wants you to expect to be blessed. If you're a Christian, you've already been blessed with every spiritual blessing in the heavenly places. If God can trust you to be generous with the earthly treasures He's given you, He will have every reason to supply you with more.

Giving is the way to receiving. Most Christians have it backward. They say, "Lord, give to me, and then I will give to You." But here is a fundamental difference between us and God: We can trust God, but He can't trust us. Many times He gives to us and never sees it again.

When we honor Him first, He promises to respond to us.

Lord, I expect to be blessed. Because of the sacrifice of Jesus Christ, You have already blessed me with every spiritual blessing in the heavenly places. My blessings are already determined and created, and they include everything. I ask for my blessings for my marriage. I ask for my spouse's blessings in Jesus's name. I expect to receive these blessings every day. I expect this because of Your Word, which is true.

You are blessed, my God, and it is Your character to bless. I hold out to You the open hands of my heart and ask You to show mercy and to fill them with blessings for my marriage. Make us smile because of Your gracious blessings. I praise You in advance. In Christ's name, amen.

The Sword of the Spirit

You shall remember the LORD your God, for it is He who is giving you power to make wealth, that He may confirm His covenant which He swore to your fathers, as it is this day.

DEUTERONOMY 8:18

According to Deuteronomy 8:18, God gives His people the power to increase through financial and spiritual blessings. God isn't against prosperity, but He is against wasting it or letting it rule our lives. He wants us to use what we have for His glory and purposes. But the question is, can He trust us with more? Are we honoring Him with what we have right now?

What you do with what you have will influence the level of your blessing.

Lord, thank You for the power You have given to us to increase and generate wealth. Thank You for the skills, talents, and interests You have placed in our lives. Thank You for the confirming love that comes to us through Your many blessings. When Satan tries to deceive us into believing that You are against prosperity and wealth, I remind him, through Jesus's name, of Deuteronomy 8:18. I remember You, for You are our Lord and our God. And I humbly submit my marriage to You in glad expectation for the myriad of blessings, both tangible and intangible, that You are readily giving to us.

Show us how to better use the blessings You have given us to help minister to others and bless them as well. Show us how to best use the influence You have given to us to point people toward You. Sharpen our skills, increase our desire, strengthen our motivation, and empower our work—done in Your name—to bring about Your intended results. And bless us relationally with mutual respect, honor, and delight as we enjoy Your blessings. In Christ's name, amen.

14

PROTECTION

The Belt of Truth

We know that no one who is born of God sins; but He who was born of God keeps him, and the evil one does not touch him.

1 John 5:18

Nothing can compare to the power of God in our lives. The same power that was given to Jesus—the power to heal, comfort, release from bondage, and restore—is living inside of you and me. The crowds that followed Christ were amazed because they had never seen anything like the miracles Jesus performed.

Wherever Jesus went, people knew who He was. Even the demons knew and shook.

Dear Lord, You are the ultimate protector of all things. Satan attempts to deceive through fear and situations that cause doubt, but all things are under Your authority in the name of Jesus Christ. I speak this truth over my marriage, over our health, over our safety, over our hearts...over all. You go before and come behind, guarding our ways and making our paths straight. Forgive me, Father, when I worry about circumstances rather than putting my faith in You and the truth of Your authority and rule.

Protect our marriage. Protect both of us in the things we eat, the things we watch, the places we go, and the ways we travel. Protect us when we are out and when we are in. Protect our hearts from worry, fear, and anxiety as well. Station Your angels as guards on the four corners of our home and our property. And give us the ability to release each other into the duties and activities You have called each of us to perform. Help us never to allow Satan to use fear and doubt to hinder us from fully living out Your purpose for our lives. In Christ's name, amen.

The Breastplate of Righteousness

He who dwells in the shelter of the Most High
Will abide in the shadow of the Almighty.
I will say to the LORD, "My Refuge and my fortress,
My God, in whom I trust!"

PSALM 91:1-2

If a fisherman were to put a hook into the water all by itself, he would be waiting there a long time before anything ever took a bite. In fact, it is doubtful that anything would ever bite his hook. Instead, what the fisherman does is put a worm on the hook to deceive the fish into thinking it is getting a tasty meal.

Satan doesn't simply throw hooks out to us either. He doesn't advertise the local tavern by saying, "Come here and get drunk, become addicted to drugs or alcohol, lose your family, lead your kids into alcoholism, and throw away your future." Rather, what Satan does can be called the "foot in the door" technique. This was a common technique for traveling salesmen. They understood that if they could get potential customers to allow him to put their foot inside the door and talk about something unrelated to the sale, they would more than likely also have the sale. To do this, they diverted the potential customer's attention to something else.

Satan tries to get believers to let him into their lives little by little just like that. First, it's just a foot in the door—maybe a movie you shouldn't have watched, a conversation you shouldn't have had, or a relationship that shouldn't have been redefined in such a way. At first, it seems harmless. But as Satan makes his way in, it becomes easier to graduate to the next level and buy what he is selling.

Father, give my spouse and me wisdom and insight to recognize Satan's strategies and schemes before they take root in our lives. Satan is a deceiver, and You say in Your Word that our hearts are deceitful above all else. Based on those two things alone, it is evident that we need Your Spirit to give us discernment on a moment-by-moment basis.

Keep us from the traps of the enemy. Help us to speak in love when one of us sees the other being lured into a potential trap or sin. Help my spouse not to be offended when I bring it up, and help me not to be offended when he/she brings it up. Rather, help both of us to have ears to hear. We must humble ourselves under You to live righteously in You. In Christ's name, amen.

The Shoes of Peace

Let the peace of Christ rule in your hearts, to which indeed you were called in one body; and be thankful.

COLOSSIANS 3:15

I wish I could tell you that when you follow Jesus, you'll never have to face any storms. I wish I could tell you that when you follow Jesus, the waters of life will always be calm. I wish I could tell you that when you follow Jesus, life will be rosy and all of your days as a married couple will be sweet. But I can't.

Jesus's disciples were obeying Him when they ran into rough seas. The disciples discovered, as many of us have also discovered, that you can be in the center of God's will and still run into a storm.

Some preachers and Christian authors will tell you that if you follow Jesus, you will never have to face any challenges in life or in your marriage. That wasn't true for Jesus or any of His followers that I know of. When we follow Jesus, we aren't immune from troubles, but we can experience His presence and peace in the midst of the trouble.

Life comes with troubles regardless of whether you follow Jesus. The question is, do you want His peace in the midst of them, or would you rather go it alone?

Lord, life comes with troubles. It does for everyone. We are not the only married couple who experiences challenges and difficulties. How we respond to those challenges and difficulties, though, is up to us. In Your Word You tell me to let the peace of Christ rule in my heart and to be thankful.

When I don't allow peace to rule in my life or in our marriage, one of the first things to go is gratitude. It is difficult to feel and express gratitude in the midst of worry, concern, or fear. So, Father, I repent for not allowing peace to rule in my heart and in my marriage. I repent of not letting gratitude fulfill its important purpose in my life and my relationships.

I pray that peace will rule in my heart and in my home. Fill my spouse and me with an overwhelming amount of gratitude. Make us a mutual-gratitude team as we look for things to be thankful for in each other and our marriage. We have so much to thank You for, Father. Thank You for reminding me of this and for Your gift of peace, which I have been called to embrace fully. In Christ's name, amen.

The Shield of Faith

He will cover you with His pinions,
And under His wings you may seek refuge;
His faithfulness is a shield and bulwark.

PSALM 91:4

> It is always best to place our faith and trust in God. No matter what the situation may be, we can't lose when the focus of our heart is set on Jesus.

Dear God, faith is one of the greatest weapons we can use in spiritual warfare to defeat the emotions of fear, anxiety, and dread. I pick up the shield of faith, trusting that my spouse and I are covered by Your protective pinions. Under Your wings we find our refuge. I place my trust in Your faithfulness because it is a shield and a bulwark. You stand watch even when I do not know to do so. You have protected our marriage in more ways than we will ever even realize. Thank You for Your ongoing protection, safety, and covering so that my spouse and I can maximize all You have created us to be both in our own lives and as a couple. In faith I choose to rest calmly rather than resort to worry. By faith I declare I am safe and my marriage is protected by You. In Christ's name, amen.

The Helmet of Salvation

You will only look on with your eyes
And see the recompense of the wicked.
For you have made the LORD, my refuge,
Even the Most High, your dwelling place.

PSALM 91:8-9

> If you feel as though you are being oppressed or depressed by the enemy, turn to the Lord. Ask Him to shine His light

on your situation and to counsel you through His Word. Nothing can compare to Jesus's wisdom and ability. The world and the enemy of our souls may try to imitate Jesus's omnipotent ability, but they cannot come close. All things in heaven and on earth are under His authority.

Lord, I look to You as the protector of our marriage. What God has brought together, nothing can separate. Not even us, Lord, when we align ourselves under Your care. I ask that You protect us, seal us, and make us one. Give us a heart of surrender, passion, and commitment for each other. Show us how to protect our eyes, ears, and hearts so that we give our best to each other. Lead us from temptation and deliver us from the evil one, for Yours is the kingdom, the power, and the glory forever. In Christ's name, amen.

The Sword of the Spirit

The thief comes only to steal and kill and destroy; I came that they may have life, and have it abundantly.

JOHN 10:10

Doppler radar makes weather patterns visible, enabling meteorologists to see something that's invisible to the eye. Doppler radar provides a measure of safety, especially at airports, where wind shears cause some pretty rough take-offs or landings.

In the spiritual realm, we're limited in our perspective. We can't see what's happening in that realm unless we believe God, who is not limited by the five senses.

If all you see about your life and surrounding circumstances is what you can see and discern, then you're missing the most important part—what is happening behind the scenes in the spiritual realm.

Lord, I rebuke the spirit of weariness and the spirit of apathy when it comes to fighting spiritual battles for the victory in my marriage. Instead, I pick up the sword of the Spirit, which is the Word of God, and agree with Your Word that Jesus came that we may have life and have it more abundantly.

I rebuke fear in Christ's name. I rebuke worry in Christ's name. I receive peace, calm, and security based on Your holy Word. May my marriage be filled with an understanding and awareness of Your abiding protection, and may we be resilient in our spirits, resisting the schemes of the enemy that weigh on us day in and day out.

Perfect love casts out fear. Your love for us and over us is perfect. Through the power of this love, I cast out fear from our hearts and our home and receive calm and gratitude. In Christ's name, amen.

15

THE HOLY SPIRIT

The Belt of Truth

When He, the Spirit of truth, comes, He will guide you into all the truth;
for He will not speak on His own initiative, but whatever He hears, He
will speak; and He will disclose to you what is to come.

JOHN 16:13

We know God wants Christians to grow. Spiritual growth takes place deep down inside us. It comes from the Holy Spirit, whose job is to make the waters flow. However, most Christians have a home-improvement mentality, depending on themselves to produce the desired development. But if we could do it ourselves, we wouldn't need the Holy Spirit. The assumption of the work of the Holy Spirit is that we can't do it ourselves. Just as air enables a horn to make a sound or wind enables a sailboat to move, the Holy Spirit enables the spiritual life to work.

Dear Lord, staying sensitive to the Holy Spirit's guidance and the words He speaks into our lives is rarely easy to do. Not because we don't want to but rather because we get caught up in the daily demands of life that distract us from our dialogue with You. But Your Holy Spirit guides us into all truth. Your Holy Spirit speaks to us what You want us to hear.

Lord, increase my intimacy with Your Spirit so that I can discern His voice easily. Increase my spouse's as well. Our marriage will thrive when we align ourselves with Your truth. Hearing from You regularly through Your Spirit is necessary for us to make wise decisions and to avoid turning onto paths that lead us nowhere. Help us to hear Your Spirit speak to us, Lord. In Christ's name, amen.

The Breastplate of Righteousness

Flee immorality. Every other sin that a man commits is outside the body, but the immoral man sins against his own body. Or do you not know that your body is a temple of the Holy Spirit who is in you, whom you have from God, and that you are not your own? For you have been bought with a price: therefore glorify God in your body.

1 CORINTHIANS 6:18-20

The very Spirit of God has taken up residence in our lives if we have accepted Jesus Christ as our Savior. God wants to express His mind, His thoughts, His desires, and His will through our mortal bodies. But for that to happen, we need to surrender to the Holy Spirit's control. While this is taking place, we are going to experience conflict within ourselves. God says the flesh and the Spirit are opposites; they're not going to get along with each other at all.

How do we know the difference between the flesh and the Holy Spirit within us? The Spirit will want to please God, and the flesh will want to please ourselves. When we submit to the Spirit's presence in our lives—meditating on the Word of God and offering praise and worship in spite of what we're feeling or experiencing—the Spirit wins out over our flesh and influences our actions.

Father, our marriage needs Your continual guidance and strength. There is a war that wages between our flesh and the Spirit You have placed within us. But You have gained the victory through Jesus Christ. Help me to be sensitive to Your Spirit's leading, knowing that I have been bought with a price and my body is Yours—I am to glorify You with my body and my choices.

I surrender my life to You, Lord, asking You to remind me that I am Yours and I am not my own. My life exists to bring You glory and to bring others good. Give me Your power to wage victorious warfare in my own life so that my spouse is ministered to by the reflection of Your wholeness in me. In Christ's name, amen.

The Shoes of Peace

The fruit of the Spirit is love, joy, peace, patience, kindness, goodness, faithfulness, gentleness, self-control; against such things there is no law.

GALATIANS 5:22-23

We all live in the flesh, so we will struggle with the desires of the flesh until we get to heaven. But we can bring these desires under the Holy Spirit's influence. "Walk by the Spirit, and you will not carry out the desire of the flesh" (Galatians 5:16). Notice that the apostle Paul doesn't say we won't *have* the desires of the flesh when we walk in the Spirit, but that we won't *carry out* those fleshly desires. Walking in the Spirit is similar to being filled with the Holy Spirit.

Walking implies that the Spirit is going somewhere—there's a *destination*. He always goes to the same place, to that which brings God glory—and much of what brings God glory is what we call the fruit of the Spirit. When this fruit is manifest in our lives, we bring God glory. In contrast, the flesh is always moving to that which will please itself. Walking is continuous. Like the filling of the Holy Spirit, our walk in the Spirit is ongoing, so we must maintain our *dedication*. To walk is to continue taking one step after another.

Lord, the fruit of Your Spirit's presence within me is love, joy, peace, patience, kindness, goodness, faithfulness, gentleness, and self-control. All of these qualities are essential to a healthy and thriving marriage. They come about through choosing to walk by the Spirit, which also means to be filled with Your Spirit. Father, I want to have Your Holy Spirit's influence in my life on such a great level that my spouse becomes the recipient of all of these character qualities Your Spirit produces in me.

I also ask that You will give my spouse the desire and discipline to be filled with Your Spirit as well. Help us both to take time to cultivate an ongoing relationship with Your Spirit. Show us the path to take that will increase our sensitivity to Your presence. Keep us from distractions that may be fun or even positive but that pull us away from Your purpose for our marriage. Help us to say no to things that will compete with our walk with the Spirit and with our investment in our marriage. Give us wisdom to discern what is of You and what is of our flesh so we can truly be filled with Your Spirit and bring You glory. In Christ's name, amen.

The Shield of Faith

Hope does not disappoint, because the love of God has been poured out within our hearts through the Holy Spirit who was given to us.

ROMANS 5:5

The Holy Spirit is the divine enabler who produces growth in us. Every time we try to grow without depending on God and exercising our faith in God, we work against Him. Many of us spend much of our time shutting God out. We're trying to produce fruit on our own. However, when we abide in Jesus Christ and the power of the Holy Spirit is the dominant influencer in our life, the fruit of the Spirit develops naturally.

Dear God, thank You for the love in our hearts that is poured out through the Holy Spirit. This love serves as the impetus for increased faith and a sustained hope. I pray that You will open our hearts as a couple all the more to allow the Holy Spirit's ever-present and perfect love to become our own, not only for each other but also for ourselves. Demonstrate in us and through us to each other the beauty of a love rooted in You.

Thank You for the confidence, based on Your Word, that hope placed in You does not disappoint. This is a hope I can cling to when things look chaotic in our relationship or our world. Let my mind remain set on You and the hope of Your calling so that my words and actions reflect a life lived in deep connection with Your Spirit. Give my spouse an increased understanding and awareness of Your Spirit's presence in me, and let that grow into a greater appreciation as well. Thank You for being the root of all good things in our relationship, and thank You for the gift of Your Spirit, who sustains us in Your love. In Christ's name, amen.

The Helmet of Salvation

In Him, you also, after listening to the message of truth, the gospel of your salvation—having also believed, you were sealed in Him with the Holy Spirit of promise.

EPHESIANS 1:13

The Holy Spirit within us makes life real; life comes alive. When we have accepted Jesus as our Savior and Redeemer, life is no longer simply theology. The theology in our heads becomes real in our lives, drawing us closer to God through the Holy Spirit. When the Holy Spirit takes over, we begin to grow. The Holy Spirit becomes the power source behind this growth so that it eventually becomes evident.

Lord, through Christ's sanctifying work on the cross, I am sealed in You with the Holy Spirit of promise. Thank You for this gift, which enables me to communicate with You and discern spiritual truths. Please help us to allow the Holy Spirit to become more and more the power source in our growth as individuals and as a couple. Let the theology we learn and hear taught to us become real in our lives. Let us live out what it means to love, care, exhort, encourage, and bless each other. Let us experience the power of Your purpose being made manifest in and through each of us. Draw us closer to You, God, through Your Holy Spirit, and let the Spirit take over our thoughts, decisions, and desires. We desire You and want to know You more. Satisfy this desire with Your presence, power, and pure love. In Christ's name, amen.

The Sword of the Spirit

The Helper, the Holy Spirit, whom the Father will send in My name, He will teach you all things, and bring to your remembrance all that I said to you.

JOHN 14:26

We can be certain that Satan knows the Bible. He knows what it says, and he also knows how to twist it into half-truths to serve his purposes. Satan can easily pull a word from God out of context—just as he did with Eve.

It isn't enough for us to know the words in the Bible; we need to know the context. We need to understand the basic principle that the Word of God never violates: God doesn't contradict Himself.

The Bible is your sword. An unpracticed swordsman will fall victim every time to someone who wields the sword more effectively. Learn how to wield your sword when the enemy takes Scripture out of context and uses it against you. Fill your heart with God's promises and take God at His Word.

Lord, Satan is a deceiver—and a clever one. The devil uses Your Word against You when he takes it out of context. Father, please give my spouse and me wisdom and insight to discern the truth and to be aware of Satan's schemes. Cover both of us with the protecting blood of Jesus Christ, especially as we approach Your Word to study and learn. When we disagree with each other about Your Word and what it means for our lives, I pray that You will bring us together in unity and understanding through the power of Your Spirit. Adam and Eve struggled to understand and live out Your word, Lord, and it cost them a lot. Let this not be so for me and my spouse. Let us stay tethered to Your truth and mindful of misinterpretations of Scripture that would divert and distract us from living according to Your will.

Thank You for the Helper, the Holy Spirit, who teaches us all things. I pray that the Holy Spirit will bring to my remembrance all that I need to know and pray about regarding my marriage. May the powerful teaching of Your Spirit in my life be evident in my marriage. Thank You. In Christ's name, amen.

DR. TONY EVANS AND THE URBAN ALTERNATIVE

About Dr. Tony Evans

Dr. Tony Evans is founder and senior pastor of the 10,000-member Oak Cliff Bible Fellowship in Dallas, founder and president of The Urban Alternative, chaplain of the NBA's Dallas Mavericks, and author of many books, including *Destiny* and *Victory in Spiritual Warfare*. His radio broadcast, *The Alternative with Dr. Tony Evans*, can be heard on more than 1000 outlets and in more than 100 countries.

The Urban Alternative

The Urban Alternative (TUA) equips, empowers, and unites Christians to impact individuals, families, churches, and communities through a thoroughly kingdom agenda worldview. In teaching truth, we seek to transform lives.

The core cause of the problems we face in our personal lives, homes, churches, and societies is a spiritual one; therefore, the only way to address it is spiritually. We've tried a political, social, economic, and even a religious agenda.

It's time for a kingdom agenda—the visible manifestation of the comprehensive rule of God over every area of life.

The unifying, central theme of the Bible is the glory of God and the advancement of His kingdom. This is the conjoining thread from

Genesis to Revelation—from beginning to end. Without that theme, the Bible becomes disconnected stories that are inspiring but seem to be unrelated in purpose and direction. The Bible exists to share God's movement in history to establish and expand His kingdom, highlighting the connectivity throughout, which is the kingdom. Understanding that increases the relevancy of these ancient writings to our day-to-day living because the kingdom is not only then; it is now.

The absence of the kingdom's influence in our own lives and in our families, churches, and communities has led to a catastrophic deterioration in our world.

- People live segmented, compartmentalized lives because they lack God's kingdom worldview.

- Families disintegrate because they exist for their own satisfaction rather than for the kingdom.

- Churches have limited impact because they fail to comprehend that the goal of the church is not to advance the church itself, but the kingdom.

- Communities have nowhere to turn to find real solutions for real people who have real problems, because the church has become divided, ingrown, and powerless to transform the cultural landscape in any relevant way.

The kingdom agenda offers us a way to live with a solid hope by optimizing the solutions of heaven. When God and His rule are not the final and authoritative standard over all, order and hope are lost. But the reverse of that is true as well—as long as we have God, we have hope. If God is still in the picture, and as long as His agenda is still on the table, it's not over.

Even if relationships collapse, God will sustain you. Even if finances dwindle, God will keep you. Even if dreams die, God will revive you. As long as God and His rule guide your life, family, church, and community, there is always hope.

Our world needs the King's agenda. Our churches need the King's agenda. Our families need the King's agenda.

In many major cities, drivers can take a loop to get to the other side of the city without driving straight through downtown. This loop takes them close enough to the city to see its towering buildings and skyline, but not close enough to actually experience it.

This is precisely what our culture has done with God. We have put Him on the "loop" of our personal, family, church, and community lives. He's close enough to be at hand should we need Him in an emergency, but far enough away that He can't be the center of who we are.

Sadly, we often want God on the "loop" of our lives, but we don't always want the King of the Bible to come downtown into the very heart of our ways. Leaving God on the "loop" brings about dire consequences, as we have seen in our own lives and with others. But when we make God and His rule the centerpiece of all we think, do, and say, we experience Him in the way He longs for us to.

He wants us to be kingdom people with kingdom minds set on fulfilling His kingdom purposes. He wants us to pray as Jesus did—"Not my will, but Thy will be done." Because His is the kingdom, the power, and the glory.

There is only one God, and we are not Him. As King and Creator, God calls the shots. Only when we align ourselves underneath His comprehensive hand will we access His full power and authority in our lives, families, churches, and communities.

As we learn how to govern ourselves under God, we will transform the institutions of family, church, and society according to a biblically based, kingdom worldview. Under Him, we touch heaven and change earth.

To achieve our goal, we use a variety of strategies, approaches, and resources for reaching and equipping as many people as possible.

Broadcast Media

Millions of individuals experience *The Alternative with Dr. Tony Evans*, a daily broadcast playing on nearly 1000 radio outlets and in more than 100 countries. The broadcast can also be seen on several television networks, online at TonyEvans.org, and on the free Tony Evans app. More than four million message downloads occur each year.

Leadership Training

The *Tony Evans Training Center (TETC)* facilitates educational programming that embodies the ministry philosophy of Dr. Tony Evans as expressed through the kingdom agenda. The training courses focus on leadership development and discipleship in five tracks:

- Bible and theology

- personal growth

- family and relationships

- church health and leadership development

- society and community impact

The TETC program includes courses for both local and online students. Furthermore, TETC programming includes course work for nonstudent attendees. Pastors, Christian leaders, and Christian laity, both local and at a distance, can seek out the Kingdom Agenda Certificate for personal, spiritual, and professional development. Some courses qualify for continuing education credits and will transfer for college credit with our partner schools.

Kingdom Agenda Pastors (KAP) provides a viable network for likeminded pastors who embrace the kingdom agenda philosophy. Pastors have the opportunity to go deeper with Dr. Tony Evans as they are given greater biblical knowledge, practical applications, and resources to impact individuals, families, churches, and communities. KAP welcomes senior and associate pastors of all churches. KAP also offers an annual summit, held each year in Dallas, with intensive seminars, workshops, and resources.

Pastors' Wives Ministry, founded by Dr. Lois Evans, provides counsel, encouragement, and spiritual resources for pastors' wives as they serve with their husbands in the ministry. A primary focus of the ministry is the KAP Summit, which offers senior pastors' wives a safe place to reflect, renew, and relax along with training in personal development, spiritual growth, and care for their emotional and physical well-being.

Community Impact

National Church Adopt-A-School Initiative (NCAASI) empowers churches across the country to impact communities by using public schools as the primary vehicles for effecting positive social change in urban youth and families. Leaders of churches, school districts, faith-based organizations, and other nonprofit organizations are equipped with the knowledge and tools to forge partnerships and build strong social service delivery systems. This training is based on the comprehensive church-based community impact strategy conducted by Oak Cliff Bible Fellowship. It addresses such areas as economic development, education, housing, health revitalization, family renewal, and racial reconciliation. We assist churches in tailoring the model to meet specific needs of their communities while simultaneously addressing the spiritual and moral frame of reference. Training events are held annually in the Dallas area at Oak Cliff Bible Fellowship.

Athlete's Impact (AI) is as an outreach into and through sports. Coaches are sometimes the most influential adults in young people's lives—even more so than parents. With the rise of fatherlessness in our culture, more young people are looking to their coaches for guidance, character development, practical needs, and hope. Athletes (professional or amateur) also influence younger athletes and kids. Knowing this, we aim to equip and train coaches and athletes to live out and utilize their God-given roles for the benefit of the kingdom. We aim to do this through our iCoach App, weCoach Football Conference, and other resources, such as *The Playbook: A Life Strategy Guide for Athletes*.

Resource Development

We are fostering lifelong learning partnerships with the people we serve by providing a variety of published materials. Dr. Evans has published more than 100 unique titles (booklets, books, and Bible studies) based on more than 40 years of preaching. The goal is to strengthen individuals in their walk with God and service to others.

For more information and a complimentary copy of Dr. Evans's devotional newsletter,

call
(800) 800-3222

or write
TUA
PO Box 4000
Dallas TX 75208

or visit our website
www.TonyEvans.org

MORE GREAT HARVEST HOUSE BOOKS BY DR. TONY EVANS

30 Days to Overcoming Emotional Strongholds

Dr. Evans identifies the most common and problematic emotional strongholds and demonstrates how you can break free from them—by aligning your thoughts with God's truth in the Bible.

30 Days to Victory Through Forgiveness

Has someone betrayed you? Are you suffering the consequences of your own poor choices? Or do you find yourself asking God, *Why did You let this happen?* Like a skilled physician, Dr. Tony Evans leads you through a step-by-step remedy that will bring healing to that festering wound and get you back on your journey to your personal destiny.

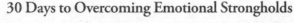

Watch Your Mouth

Your greatest enemy is actually in your mouth. Dr. Evans reveals life-changing, biblical insights into the power of the tongue and how your words can be used to bless others or to usher in death. Be challenged to use your mouth to speak life into the world around you. (Also available—*Watch Your Mouth Growth and Study Guide*, *Watch Your Mouth DVD*, and *Watch Your Mouth Interactive Workbook*.)

A Moment for Your Soul

In this uplifting devotional, Dr. Evans offers a daily reading for Monday through Friday and one for the weekend—all compact, powerful, and designed to reach your deepest need. Each entry includes a relevant Scripture reading for the day. (eBook only)

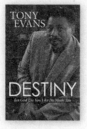

Destiny

Dr. Evans shows you the importance of finding your God-given purpose. He helps you discover and develop a custom-designed life that leads to the expansion of God's kingdom. Embracing your personal assignment from God will lead to your deepest satisfaction, God's greatest glory, and the greatest benefit to others.

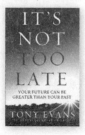

It's Not Too Late

Dr. Evans uses prominent Bible characters to show that God delights in using imperfect people who have failed, sinned, or just plain blown it. You'll be encouraged as you come to understand that God has you, too, on a path to success *despite* your imperfections and mistakes.

The Power of God's Names

Dr. Evans shows that it's through the names of God that the nature of God is revealed. By understanding the characteristics of God as revealed through His names, you will be better equipped to face the challenges life throws at you.

Praying Through the Names of God

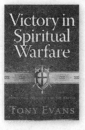

Dr. Evans reveals insights into some of God's powerful names and provides prayers based on those names. Your prayer life will be revitalized as you connect your needs with the relevant characteristics of His names.

Victory in Spiritual Warfare

Dr. Evans demystifies spiritual warfare and empowers you with a life-changing truth: Every struggle faced in the physical realm has its root in the spiritual realm. With passion and practicality, Dr. Evans shows you how to live a transformed life in and through the power of Christ's victory.

Prayers for Victory in Spiritual Warfare

Feel defeated? God has given you powerful weapons to help you withstand the onslaught of Satan's lies. This book of prayers, based on Dr. Evans's life-changing book *Victory in Spiritual Warfare*, will help you stand against the enemy's attacks.

Horizontal Jesus

Do you want to sense God's encouragement, comfort, and love for you every day? Dr. Tony Evans reveals that as you live like a horizontal Jesus—giving these things away to others—you will personally experience them with God like never before. (Also available—*Horizontal Jesus Study Guide*.)

To learn more about Harvest House books and
to read sample chapters, visit our website:

www.harvesthousepublishers.com

HARVEST HOUSE PUBLISHERS
EUGENE, OREGON